SANTA FE FOR ART'S SAKE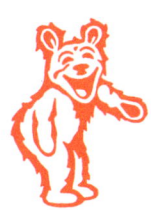

Axle Contemporary • Theater Grottesco • Burning Books • 2022

Santa Fe For Art's Sake Sake (the book)

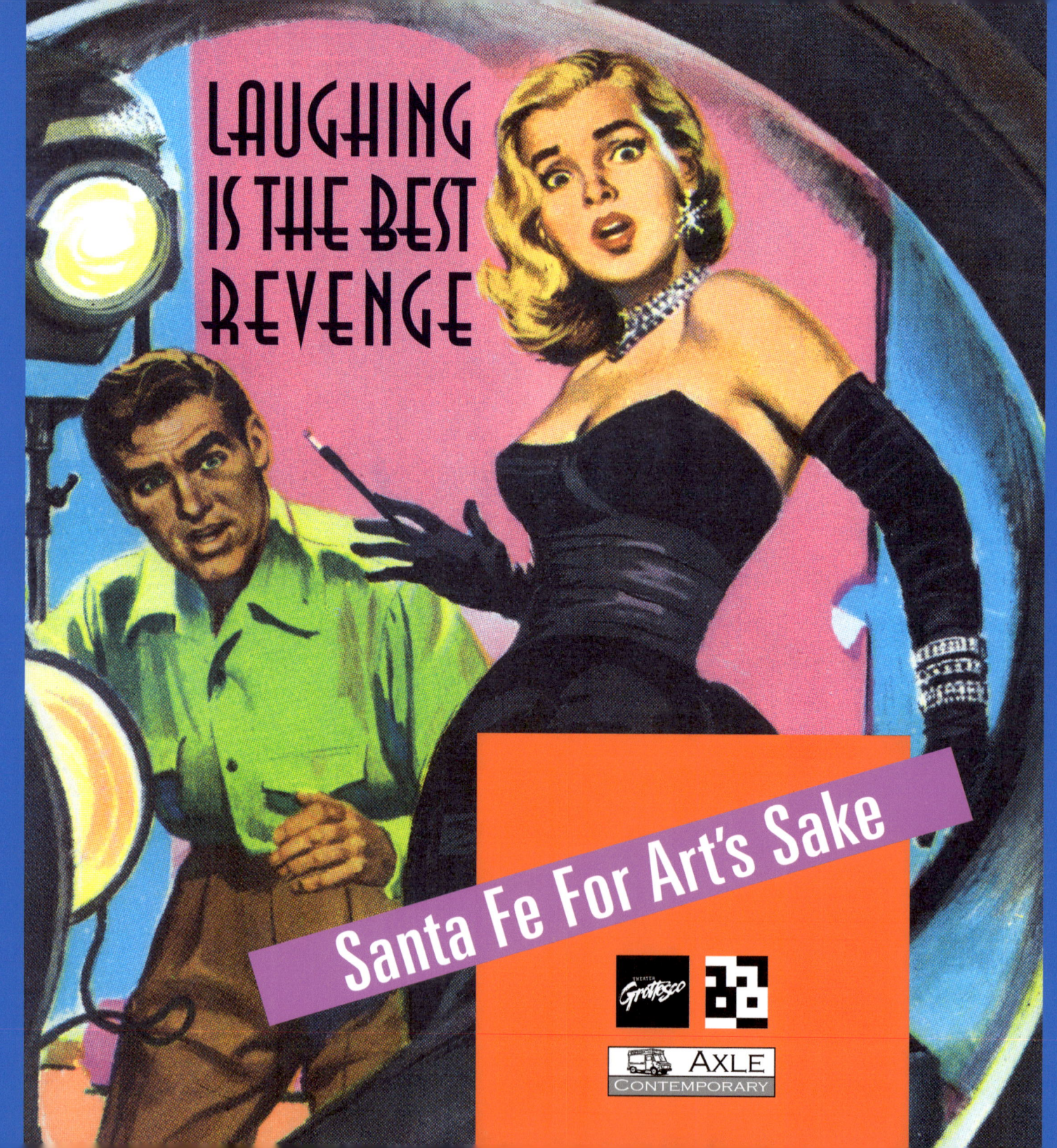

Axle Contemporary • Theater Grottesco • Burning Books

Santa Fe For Art's Sake treats the "survey" as a new form for generating experimental theater and visual art. Bouncing between the absurd and the suddenly profound, questions and answers address topics relevant to the arts and culture of Santa Fe, New Mexico, while engaging nationally and internationally with generous respondents.

Part One was an interactive and irreverent online survey, created by Burning Books, in which people were asked to answer sometimes serious, sometimes skewed, questions alongside surprising historical facts.

Part Two is a presentation of the survey results on the outside and inside of Axle Contemporary mobile art space with a dismantling of gravitas by an analysis of social media activities—including pie charts, video, and wheat paste to "post" additional graphics.

Part Three involves diverse dramatic presentations throughout New Mexico by Theater Grottesco in which the questions and answers serve as prompts to the performances, and the survey itself is turned into biting theatrical events presented live and recorded.

Part Four is the online dissemination of recordings of the dramatic plays, including graphic backdrops by Axle and Burning Books. This book is a distillation of the "greatest hits" from the (unedited) survey responses, as well as some pertinent background information with, hopefully, a few entertaining facets of today's inscrutable world.

WHAT BOOK CONNECTS THESE TWO MEN?

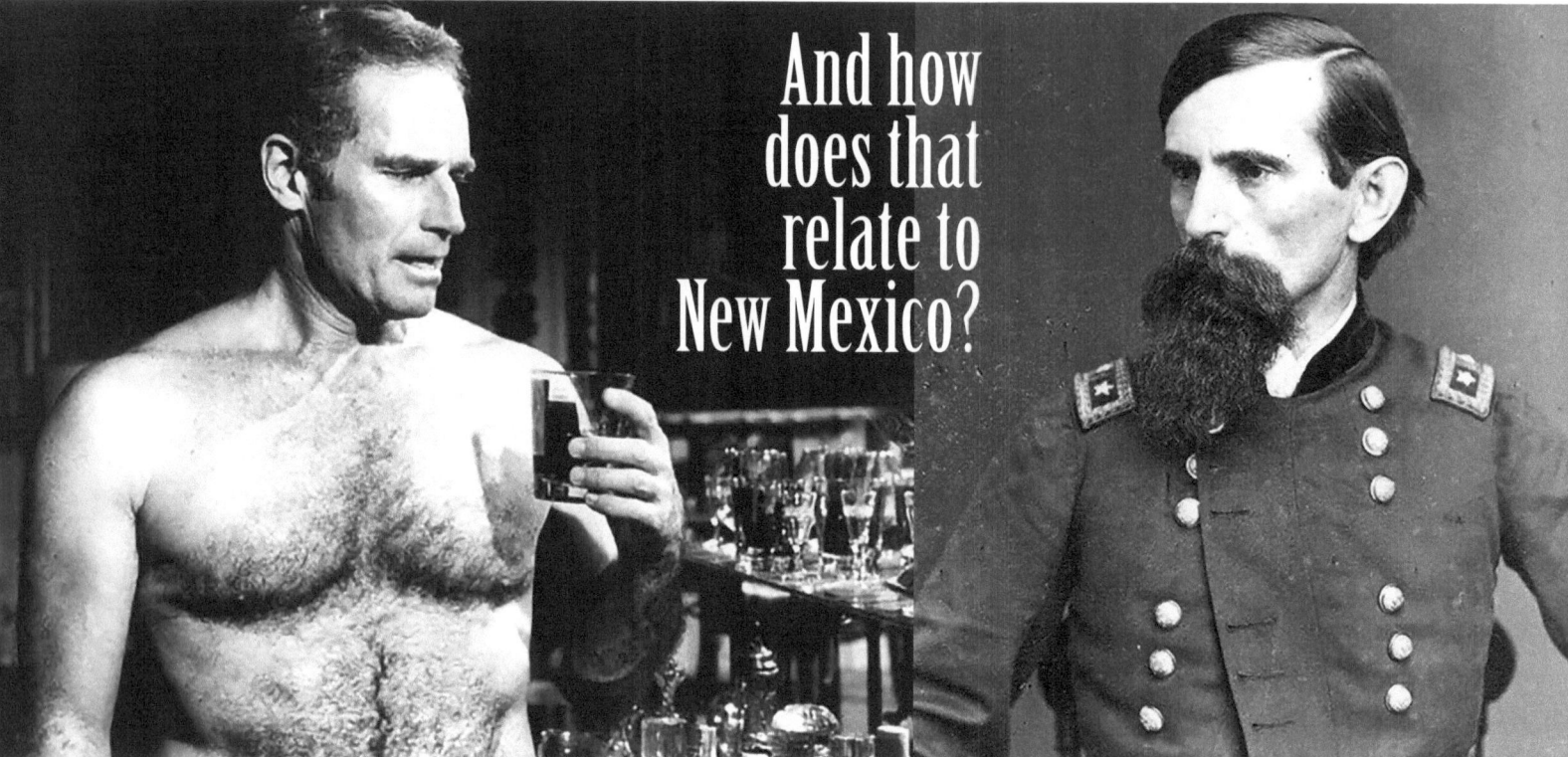

And how does that relate to New Mexico?

a movie?

Absolutely no clue

And you EXPECT me to know the answer to this? All I can think of is "The Bible"...

Autumn of the Patriarch – reflects NM's settler colonial past/ present.

beats me

Beh Hur

Ben Hur [the correct answer— *25 times*]

Ben Hur – A Tale of the Christ written by Lee Wallace! Heston later stared in the movie!

ben hur -- no particular relationship to nm other than maybe the author lived here. story somebody made up

ben hur -- written by lew wallace when in the gov's office starring charlton heston

Ben Hur by Lee Wallace, guvna

Ben Hur written by Lew Wallace a former govenor of New Mexico territory. I live on Lew Wallace Drive once upon a time. It's the only reason I know.

Ben Hur written by Lew Wallace, former governor of NM, Charleton Heston stars in the 1959 Hollywood movie.

Ben Hur written by Lew Wallis when he was Governor of the Territory of NM

Ben hur, but i had to google

Ben Hur, it doesn't relate, should it?

Ben Hur, written in New Mexico

Ben Hur? Lew Wallace? Charlton Heston?

Ben Hur. Guv Lew Wallace wrote the book

Ben Hur ... maybe. And who actually IS that second guy?? Guessing Lew Wallace very disliked by the Santa Fe Ring!!!

Ben-Hur

Ben-Hur, because the author was the governor.

Ben-Hur, written by a governor of NM. **Mr Wallace does not have that much hair on his chest, though.**

Ben-Hur: A Tale of the Christ was written by Lew Wallace, territorial governor of New Mexico, who famously said "all calculations based on experience elsewhere, fail in New Mexico."

Ben-Hur! Written by our first (I think?) Governor

Blood and Thunder

Blood and Thunder :)

Blood and thunder, fur trapping

Blood and Thunder?

6

Blood, Thunder and Apes

Brave new world, colonialism and dystopia

Cat on a Hot Tin Roof

Cluster's last stand

Damn What have I done?

Dark and swarthy

Das Boot

Don't know?

dont know dont care

Dunno

Dunno

Good one. First I was thinking Civil War and Major Dundee, but then I remembered former NM Gov. Lew Wallace wrote "Ben-Hur," which became a movie starring Charlton Heston.

Good question

Governor Lew Wallace wrote Ben Hur and what's his faced starred in the movie.

Grooming Options for the Rugged Man available at Collected Works in Santa Fe.

Hairy men of the US

Harry Potter. Because they have hair. **And you asked and you're in New Mexico.**

Haven't the foggiest

History of the world and everyone who ever lived and how they are "connected" by ozy mundi Ray

Hmmm ... Blood and Thunder?? Don't know

I do not know

I do not know and trying to google the answer to this doesn't seem fair.

I do not know these (seemingly) white men. I don't know most men in New Mexico, actually.

I don't know

I don't know

I don't know

I don't know

I have no clue.

Idunno

Jane Eyre. It is both men's favorite book. And few people know that Jane and Mr. Rochester moved to what is now New Mexico not long after the birth of their son.

Lew Wallace wrote Ben-Hur, and Charlton Heston played the lead in the film version. Wallace wrote part of the book while governor of the New Mexico territory.

Major Dundee

Men are from Mars ... Roswell

Men are from Mars, women are from Venus. Relates to NM traffic laws.

Movie

no idea
no idea
No idea.
... no idea.

Of course !

Officers clothed and unclothed in SF

Planet of the apes

Probably something by Hemingway, he liked hairy manly men ...

Radical Republican -- and I don't know about New Mexico

re. hairy men not of Tewa pueblo

something about Lew Wallace

The AngloSaxon Male in New Mexico: An Ethnographic Study

The Bible

The Bible

The Bible and this is holy land

The bible. According to everyone, it all started "here" — "here" being wherever one is.

the Bible. Both misunderstood it and acted badly as a result.

The Bible. Too many Christians.

The city charter

The Encyclopedia Britannica

The good, the bad, and the ugly. probably. It's related because it happened at a place, and New Mexico is also a place

the good, the bad, and the ugly

The Grapes of Wrath — Heston is drinking grape juice and Lew Wallace's middle name was Grape

The Gunning of America: Business and the Making of American Gun Culture. Relates to New Mexico because it relates to everywhere in the US, Kit Carson and Charlton Heston two of guns' disciples.

the hitchhikers guide to the galaxy

The Hunger Games. They were the tributes from New Mexico.

The I Ching

The Joy of Sex. People have sex in NM.

The man on the right is Lew Wallace, governor of New Mexico and also author of the epic Ben-Hur. The man on the left is the starring actor in the film adaptation of Ben-Hur.

The novel, Ben Hur was written by NM Territorial Governor Lew Wallace and published in 1880. The 1959 film starred Charleton Heston in the title role.

the pastafarian bible

The Roaches Have No King

The Swimmer

The Tibetan Book of the Dead, which they carried in their saddlebags and sold door to door through Santa Fe. They sold two copies each.

They both have long, pointy noses and enjoy being photographed in profile

two men

"Thinking of Something Else." It does not relate to New Mexico

wallace was governor of nm

We Love Tequila

What is a "book"?

White patriarchal hate

White trash

Who cares they are just two most likely dead white guys.

Why Jackets Are are a "Must Have" at Formal Dinners, by Emily Post.

Why?

Your moms box on vacation in NM

WHICH cliché says it all, based on your own gestalt of the moment?

naked power grab (10.8%)
caught flat-footed (0.6%)
at the end of my rope (15%)
writing's on the wall (15%)
take the bull by the horns (14%)
pay through the nose (3.6%)
by the skin of my teeth (13.8%)

a stitch in time saves nine
all hat no cowboy
another day another dollar
Aye, aye aye
birds of a feather
by the hair on my chinny chin chin
Capitalism Kills
cat's out of the bag
caught flat-footed
clusterfuck? four horsemen? perfect storm?
do be do be do
Down for the Count.
everything is temporary
Free floating
Happy as a clam
hard to know anymore
Hope springs eternal
I'm stuck in the upside down, please for the love of god call Nancy and Steve
keep on keeping on
life is good
Manana
Meaner than a striped rattle snake
no use crying over spilt milk
none of the above
One step at a time!
passing through the eye of the needle...
Pay it forward
Putting one foot in front of the other
que chingada
round and round we go
ship has sailed
Stitch in time saves nine
superette
Surveys are meaningful
Take the power of the rope by the writing of my nose
Takes one to know one
Too good to be true
Too woke for me
Up shit creek
We gotta get outta this place if it's the last thing we ever do.
what's a gestalt? I have one? OMGus now my paradigm itches
Whatever!
Wired and inspired
You can't get blood out of a turnip
You don't say
You reap what you sow

WHICH of the following describes you in a social situation?

— poised and self-assured (14%)
— untidy, too conspicuous (1.8%)
— rambling, disorganized (5.3%)
— keen but reticent (29.8%)
— well-adjusted but immature (7.6%)
— dominates the conversation (0%)
— ill at ease (11.1%)

26 feet away
absent
acting contagious
all of the above
Awful
Awkward and quiet
Blunt and on point
both rambling/disorganized and ill at ease
Calm
Can't really remember but I think, anxious for it to end and surprised when it goes alright
charming, brilliant, but not too dominant
Contingent
curious
depending on the group, could be any of the above.
Depends on the social situation
Different
Eccentric, eclectic, artist
enthusiastic, but unaware of how it's received
esoteric and irreverent
focused and bored or turned on and reluctant
frightened like a first-grader until I find a kindred spirit or interesting conversationalist
generally comfortable
hahaha
ill at ease, keen but reticent, rambling, and disorganized
interested
Listening from the periphery
Masked and ready
Must be perfect. Must be perfect. Mst b prftc.
not fully present
Orson Welles, without the wine
poet laureate
positive and awkward with a dash of dorky
raucous and invisible
regretting hugging people who are uncomfortable hugging
Talks long enough to confuse everyone and gain a stalker.
Timid yet self assured
Unhinged, but secretly
What - exactly - is a social situation?
What social situations ---
What's a social situation?
While feeling old and over.
you can only choose one!?

Possible "alternate career paths" chosen by our survey takers:

- **augmented reality journey builder (15.5%)**
- **inventive catenator (13%)**
- **juvenile cybercrime rehabilitation counselor (8.7%)**
- **metaversifier (5%)**
- **multi-minimizer (8.1%)**
- **personal data broker (1.9%)**
- **suasive moralizer (6.8%)**
- **"other" (41%)** . . .

Astronaut
Bag lady
BD oarsman at the Ark's helm
Bocce tournament organizer
bookaroo (librarian)
Broad Geographic Coloraturist
cannot escape being an artist
cantankerous retiree
Cantankerous senior
caretaker
CEO
champion procrastinator
Dancing to my own tunes!
de-ing-ing any participles that have one
death doula
dentist
Detectorist
Dirt farmer
Extra medium
Freelance Cat herder
Garbage man
heavy cruft-switcher
human being
i sell tickets for people to access the analog world again :)
I want to be an Artist (when I grow up … I am 69)
Influencer
jargon translator
lie-detector
literature cross-indexer
matchmaker, herbalist, seamstress, writer
Member of Anonymous
Mortality educator (you could die— you really could).
Mounted archer
Nomadic cat herder
None of the above
Noticer (unpaid)
organic farmer
Pickleball champion.
plumber
Pocket Gopher Translation Specialist
Recondite influencer
respirateur
rock star
rural rationizer
shape shifter
Slouch
Solar panel salesman
Something about medicinal soup?
Spacial genius or radiologist or anesthesiologist
Surgeon, any type
Theater person
time traveler
travel photographer
vibe curator
void starer
walmart greeter
what???
working
writer
Young Santa impersonator

Some people say Santa Fe is very woo-woo.

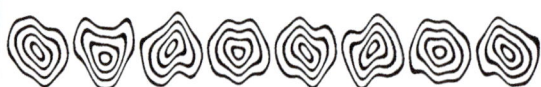

What is *woo-woo*?

A belief in things that can't been seen or explained. Crystal vibrations, aural emanations, spirit guidance, vibrational healing, and the HUM

A bit full of itself, sometimes. Other places in the state are great too!

A celestial vibration

A lady wearing hemp fabric clothes smelling like essential oils breaks away from her drum circle on the plaza to rub a crystal on you and you say thank you and leave unfazed.

A psuedo mysticism

a sexual organ

A spiritual place that not everyone gets.

a state of being open to other dimensions and spirits

A term used when having fun. Ex. "I was on the squire but zipper and when if flipped around I was like woo-woo!"

a town called "Pretension"

A vegan temptation

Accepting deep metaphysical ideas and beliefs

According to Zane, me

Actually, Sedona, AZ, is very woo-woo.

Affected, trendily artificial, shi-shi

airy-fairy

airy-fairy pseudo-spiritual

fluffiness. I think we've recently outsourced much of Santa Fe's woo-wooness to Sedona, Arizona.

alt spiritualism, herblism, & approriated shamaniic elitism

Alternative beliefs

Alternative beliefs (holistic remedies, homeopathic remedies, etc)

An excitable confusion that brings out the feeling in you that makes you notice only art and the mood it brings woo wooo

An herbal celebration

an over reliance on the supernatural and metaphysical world

anything that repeats twice to make a silly phonetic sound

arty farty newage some kind of spiritual

being a little dipherent, unconventional, searching without necessarily finding, wandering and maybe or maybe not being lost, being attuned to energies that many other people don't perceive, wallpapering over your loneliness and white privilege with various 'spiritual' trappings

believing in magic

Believing that crystals will cure your herpes.

boo-hoo dancing

Bullshit

Bullshit alternative healer spiritual white people crap. Dimming down anything that's difficult ineffable or hard work and turning it into superficial crap

Connected to the spiritual realm

Connected to the subconscious.

contemporary new age cosmopolitan

cosmic and pretentious

crazy

Crazy

Crunchy

Delightfully different

Depends on who 'SOME PEOPLE' are . . . .

different, interested in the bizarre and spiritual, spacey and ungrounded

disconnected from reality

Dunno

Earth muffin-y

Eccentric

Ego mixed with money

Either holistic or Fringe lunatic depending on context

Everyone in Santa Fe

EXCITED

Extraordinary, mystical, spiritual, unconventional in their thinking and beliefs

Fancy train

Fancy.

Faux spiritual

Fiscally conservative neoliberal Texans and New Yorkers that come to the desert with too much money, no class analysis, an interest in "energy work", and a passion for objectifying and commodifying Indigenous culture

Full of mysticism is woo-woo.

Fun

Great spirit and atmosphere

high-frequency vibes

hippie dippie silly willy

Hippie dippie, spiritual-ish, wisdom of the burnt out

Hippy

Hippy dippy new age tin foil hat

hippy dippy tin foil

hippy-dippy

hipster airy fairy

ho ho

How many of your personalities are here right now?

In and out of the ordinary, i.e. everything

Isn't it spiritual crystal healing hippie types?

It is.

It's a term used by squares to explain why they can't understand artist types …

It's like, when your VW van breaks down and you look around in your stoned state and think "COOL, I think I'll stay here and become a therapist or real estate agent."

It's out there.

Just a little left of center

Kind of like…vaguely conspiracy theory, snake oil, New Age, occultish, "not religious but spiritual" stuff

Lights you up!

Like the Taos Hum

LOL. You have to be woo-woo to say what it means

magical and prone to new-age thinking!

Meow Wolf

my dog hungry

My theory: Woo woo is a co-opted/ politically incorrect derivation of Wu-Wei - a Chinese practice of the zen of "doing nothing." Objects and actions can have "Wu"- the character of the un pushed flow of life. wuwu being a way to reference or make fun of a more complex concept and compare it to nonsense. Blindly used by all involved, me included.

Mystical and touchy-feely

New Age

New age anti vaccine white supremacy

New age culture as it relates to ideology/conversations as well as goods and services offered.

new age to nazi pipeline

new age, spiritually ungrounded

New agey

New agey spacey

New Agey, from the musical genre vibe to a genre-bending spirituality, a macrodoser not a microdoser, hairy, sari-wearing white ladies, would-be Indigenous peaceniks, anti-historical, and either lightly educated or superovereducated, and none of this woo-woo mindset is trendy, just ongoing.....for eternity.....

New agey. Folks who are into crystals, alternative medicine, astrology. The woo-woo and the right are getting closer under the anti vax banner.

not much

Old and young simultaneously

Ooowooow

oow-oow seen from the caboose

Open to spiritual connections

open to transcendental concepts and existence

Out of touch with reality

out there

out there

out there spiritual practices

Out there...

Outside the cultural norm

Overheard in Santa Fe: "No, I don't want my aura palpated."

Overly Hollywooded

People who know stuff about stuff

physic and beyond

Privileged beliefs in lazy unfounded ideas

Proto-Goop

Pseudoscience and scams

Rich people who think they're cool for wearing turquoise and only hanging out at the plaza

Santa Fe

Snake oil

so what

spiritual

spiritual and belief of spirits and devine symbolism

Spiritual beliefs with no scientific basis.

Spiritual mumbo-jumbo, esoteric rituals w crystals and burning smelly things, astrological woo, many types of woo.

spiritual nonsense

spiritual stuff

statins and prozac in the water

The picture is worth 10,000 waves. words.

The rarified air and beautiful atmospheric color at sunset.

The sound of a coyote howling on a mesa above the wind through the piñon at solstice during a full moon.

The vibes out in the ether that either make people totally awesome, like artists, or totally annoying like the people who shop at Whole Foods and park park to save their life.

The wooiest woo

There is no real definition for woo-woo. It's a feeling you get when you look up in the sky at a chemtrail. It cannot be captured in a material object or a definition. That's woo-woo!!!

Unanswerable questions

Unconventional

unhinged

unscientific out-of-the-box jackalope fodder

Uptown with a lowtown look

using magnets on a mother to diagnose food allergies in her baby by disrupting her field -- it works!!

velvet teal coyote genre

very que fancy

vibrational

Vodka, cranberry and peach schnapps

wacky, wierd, wily, wonkers

We're on a vortex, man

Weirdly awesome

what ever you want it to be

What you hear after the (correct amount of) four chugga-chuggas.

White people's version of MOJO or the reverse of oww-oww.

Who are these "some people" isn't that more important?

who cares

Who cares

Who knew?

Wildly out there and strangely inside.

Woo woo is like choo choo without the smoke

woo woo is pretty annoying, but I think there is some weird magic in the world.

woo woo is the condition of believing you are in the most important part of the world because you are the most important person in the world, but you show it through behavior you think makes you look generous and spiritual

Woo-woo is a term often heard in Fanta Se and describes a feeling of wonder at the interconnectedness of all things.

Woo-woo is as woo-woo does

Woo-woo is uWu.

woo-woo is when a person duct tapes a crystal to a leaking gas line in their car.

woo-woo is when your ideals and values in life don't fit into the "work until you die, and all that matters is $$" value that we're taught.

woo-woo is woo-woo

Wooooooooooooo! Woo

You can do what you want!

You get a woo-woo vibe from a place. If you're a cool person, you enjoy the vibe. If you're lame, you do not.

You know it when you feel it.

You know. Woo-woo. And it's always hyphenated.

You you and mimi

you-you know-know

You'll know it when you see it

THIS is the back door of?
- 🔵 Maria's New Mexican Kitchen (7.1%)
- 🔴 Santa Fe Institute (10.9%)
- 🟢 Museum of International Folk Art (40.4%) — Partial credit. Same parking lot, wrong building.
- 🟠 The Laboratory of Anthropology (17.9%) – **correct answer**

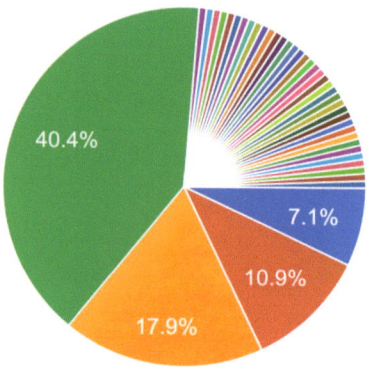

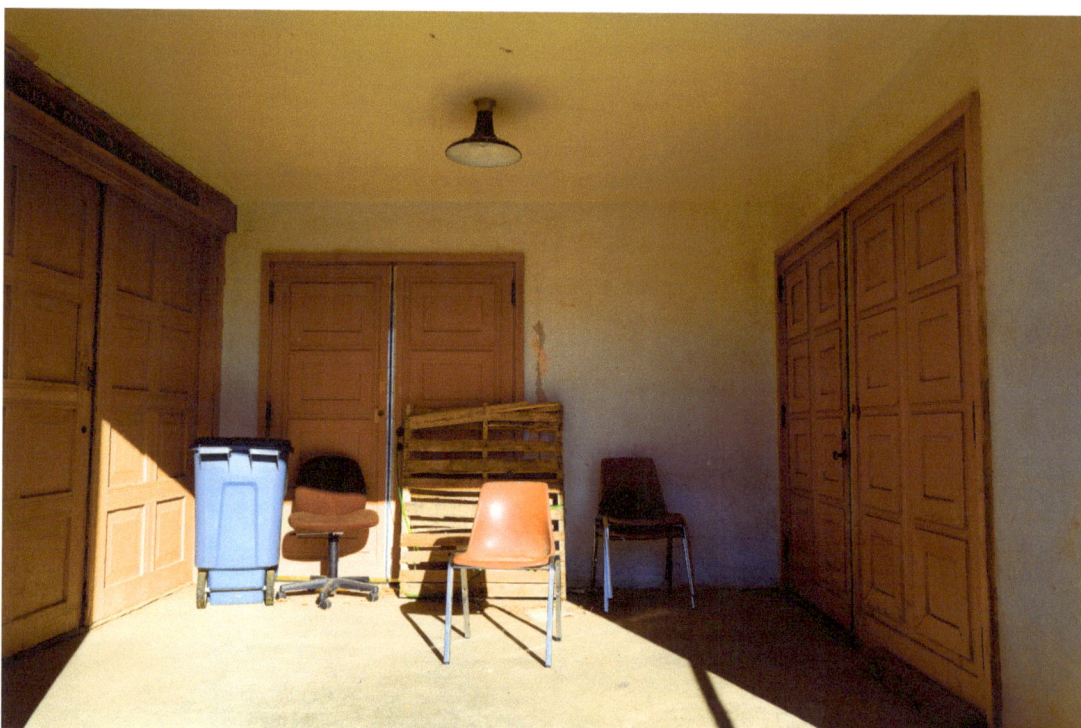

all our houses
anywhere
Area 51
Can't remeber
Counter Culture Cafe
Don't know, but I bet it's cool!
Haven't a clue…
how the hay would i know
I see six doors.
Is that my back door? Isn't it? I think it could be. I'll just go look…. I'm back… Nope, it's Lew Wallace's house.
just a guess
La Casa de Más o Menos
Matthew's house
mayor webber's office
My house
My mind
Never there………

no idea
Santa Fe
State capitol
the band room at Sante Fe High School
The Burrito Spot on Cerrillos at Lujan St.
The front of a sideways building
The House of Eternal Return. The only way to get there is by an actual, real portal.
The Mayor's Office

the metaverse
Too numerous to mention
Val Kilmers house but where's the turquoise?
…which is blocked
Who knows
Why would I know this?
Wondering how I would know???
Yes
Your mom
Your mom's house

And THIS is the back door of?
- Ten Thousand Waves (1.9%)
- Santa Fe Opera (20%)
- Scottish Rite Temple (28.7%)
- La Fonda on the Plaza (30%) – **correct answer**

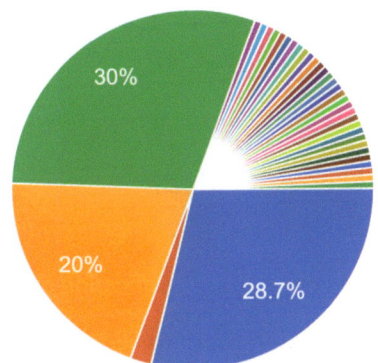

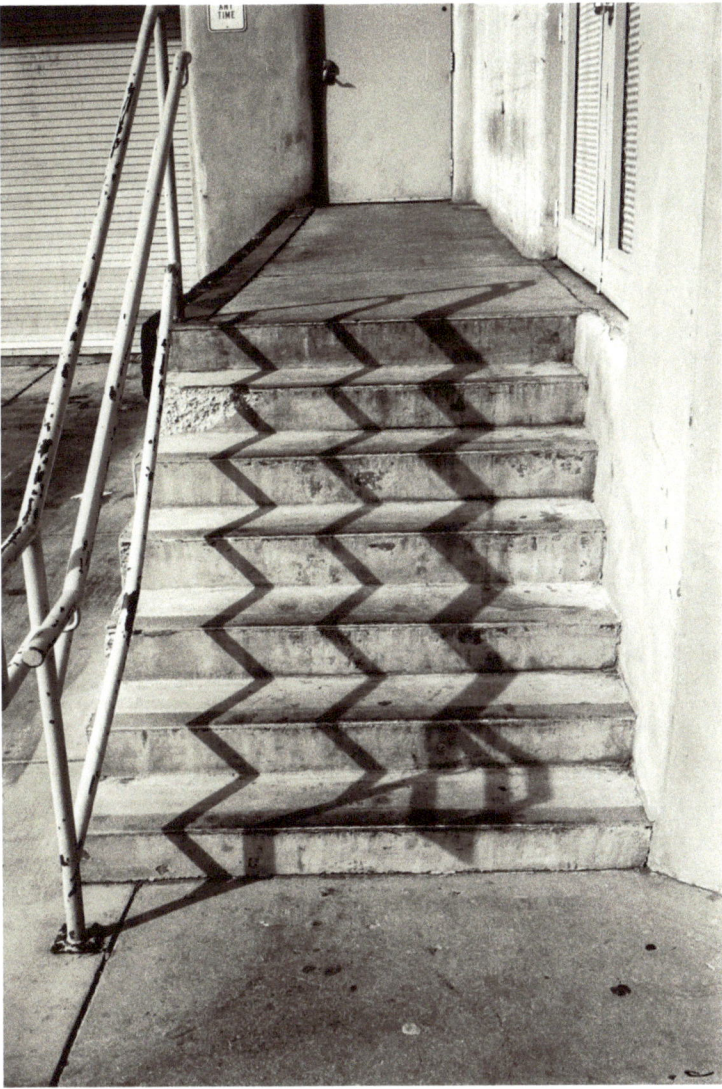

again, why the hay would i know or care
Again, why would I know this?
Also Santa Fe
Brancusi's studio in Paris
Cheeks
Don't be dirty.
El Dorado Hotel
Eldorado Hotel
Excellent question
fort mason
Heaven
Heck if I know…
I don't know
Jerry's house
just a guess
La raza
My house
no idea
Now that is my back door.
Presbyterian church
Santa Fe Humane Society; they let people take the really nervous newly-adopted dogs and cats out the back door so they don't get overwhelmed.
Site
St. Catherine's Indian School
Stairway to Heaven
the omniverse
the place with the front door
the previous place (see way above) or home
The zipper factory.
UNM fine Arts Building
Your Mamma

THIS QUESTION could contain an excessive amount of intricate detail that may interest only a particular audience.

- Face With Hand Over Mouth (11.8%)
- Face Without Mouth (11.8%)
- Face With Head-Bandage (7.9%)
- Exploding Head (34.2%)

OTHER:

a mirror

all of the above but also face with gritted teeth and face with spiral eyes and face with x-eyes

Black Hole, Los Alamos

bot fly

Burning eyeballs

cucumbers is clearly the correct answer here. I will gladly receive my 200 bitcoin now thank you

Dismayed onlooker

Duck and cover and kiss your ass goodbye device (but does it have a camera and can you get it without buying in to a "plan"?

Face with legs

Face with open mouth gasping shock

Head-scratching Face

Indeed

It's a face about an about-face.

Lewd moon

Magnum robotic condom

Man hook hand car door

Man taking picture

No head and two legs.

Nuclear Device

Person standing farther away with the floor behind them looking like shoulders

Person standing with a yellow object in hand. No face visible.

Pokémon with bolo tie man

Reflection selfie

Replica that was too replica-ish and should have been classified

Shrunken Head

something very bad

Squid or catfish

The National Museum of Nuclear Science and History?

Tube with intent to kill

unrecognizable corpses

What is the question?

14

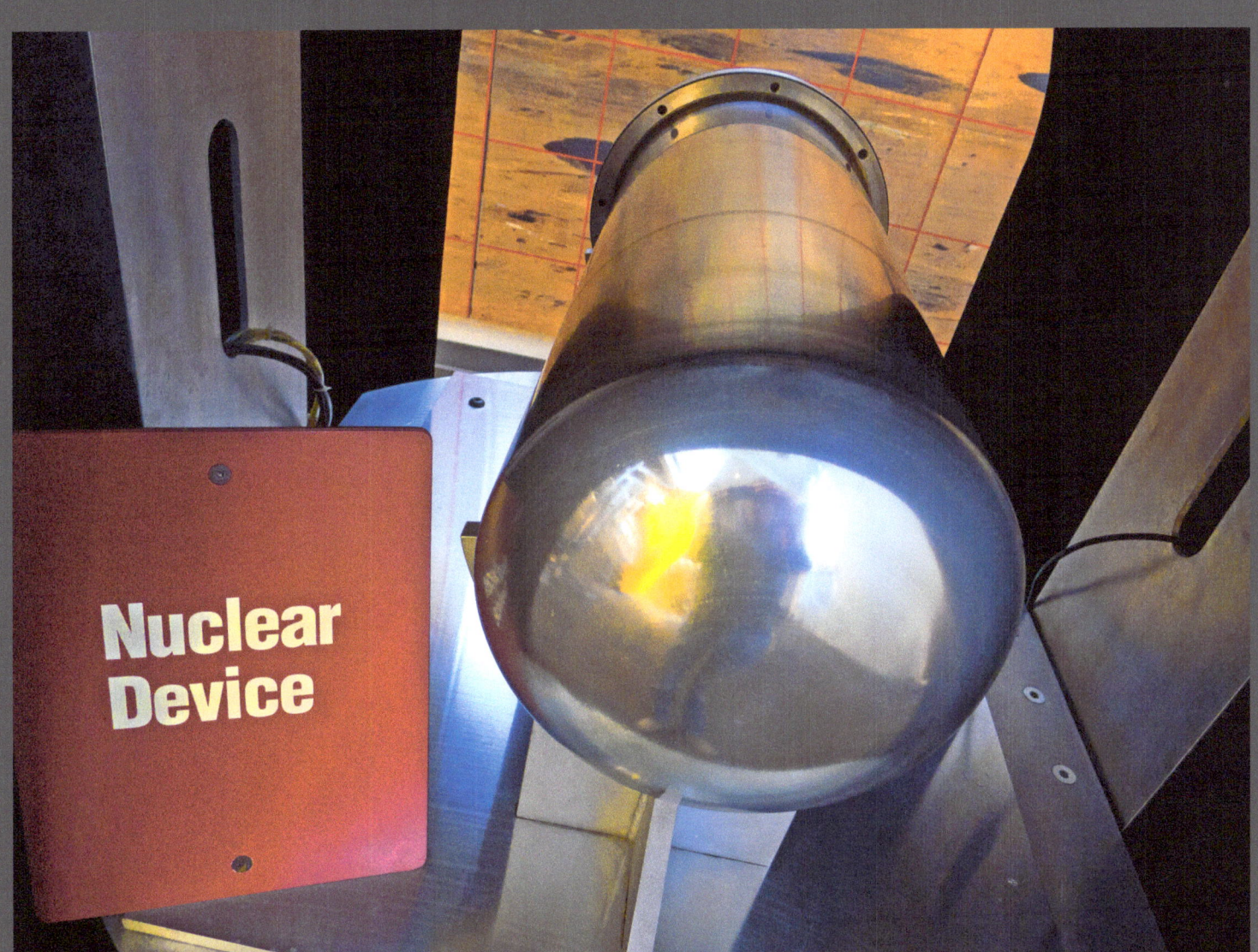

WHAT breaks your heart again and again until it stays open?

a defibrillator

a good sunset

A knife, ice pick, or something else sharp

Abandoned animals

An open mind keeps you from a broken heart.

Art

Baby kittens

being loved when you don't feel you deserve it

boys

Bullshit

Call the Midwife

Capitalism

Catharsis

Cats dressed in clown outfits

Children

Chocolate, tacos, and tequila

cholesterol

climate change & exxon mobil sponsoring the balloon fiesta

Climate denial

cluelessness

compassion

coronary infarction

Dads.

death

Death.

either life or that carnival ride

Extinctions

Flower-Petal Rib-Cage, let me bloom for you. –A. Sleep

God

God ... according to Hazrat Inayat Khan

gratitude

Green Chile

Grief

Hate

hatred

Hmmmmmm.......hate and ignorance (sort of)

Hope

Huh?

Inequity

kids

kids making discoveries

La Vie En Rose

Life

life

Live Performance

loss

Love [17 times]

love ~ in a good way

love . . .

loving other people, losing them

luv

My cat

My children

My children, my husband, my dog, a good book

My dad?

My family, my needs and my inability to recognize and meet them

My kids, music, certain Rothko paintings.

my mind

my wife's heart
Nina Simone

nothing

nothing

oh my god. Brownsville girl. bartending. love and death.

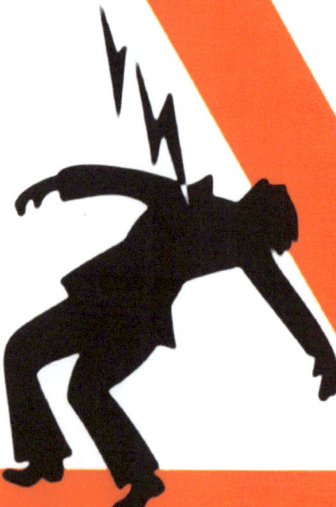

Ojo Caliente hot springs

Old age

other people

Pasqual's

People

People pushing at my boundaries

People, man. People are capable of so goddamned much, but only ever seem to lean into hateful destructive garbage on any real scale.

People's refusal to take responsibility for their own choices

Petrichor

Poetry, good lighting

Polar bears

Prefer not to answer

Prejudice

Questionnaires as art

questions

Raising my wonderful amazing son.

relationships

Relationships and vulnerability

Remembering life with my late beloved wife

Starlight in the desert.

Suffering

that we will all die

The damage humans do- to one another, to the animals, to the planet ... we are so short sighted

The death of a pet

The desert wind?

The full moon.

The illusion of separation

The inhumanity of humans, including me.

The love and joy I feel from sharing time and space with other people.

The optimism of children

The sight of people unhoused, addicted, desperate, suffering while there is so much to go around. Inequity in general.

The tantalizing longing for sisterhood.

the thought that my mother doesn't have much time left to live and we live so far apart

the vulnerable. the courage of wild life forms to persevere

The way people treat one another

violence

Waking up.

Watching children grow up

white man's cruelty to native peoples

withholding name

You presume I have a heart.

WHAT ARE YOU, PERSONALLY, MOST LIKELY TO GET ARRESTED FOR IN SANTA FE?

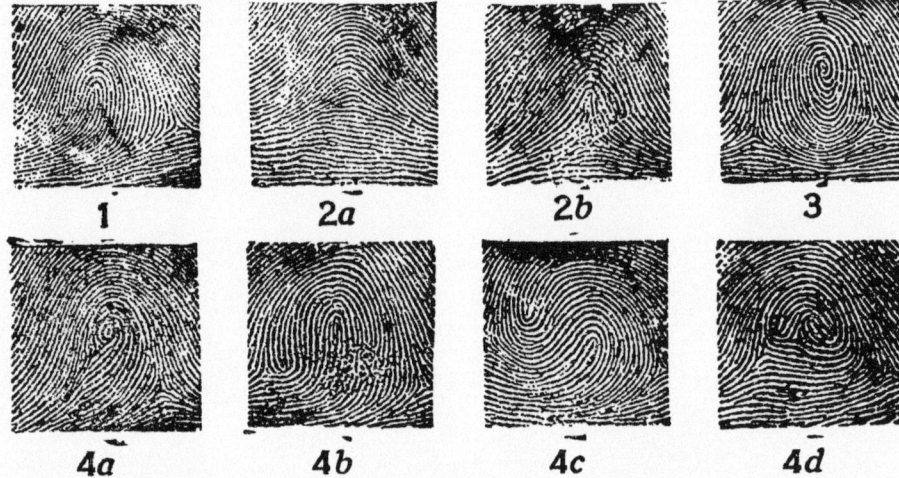

bank robbery (3.9%)
breaking and entering (3.2%)
indecent exposure (9.1%)
possession of controlled substances (16.9%)
shoplifting (10.4%)
toppling monuments (14.3%)
urinating on monuments (11.7%)
vandalizing monuments (9.1%)

anti-war demonstration
arguing over parking
assaulting tourists
Barking dog, but "bless his heart, he "caint hep" it.
Beating obnoxious people with my cane
Being brown
being devastatingly handsome while walking alone on the plaza at a reasonable hour
breathing
causing a traffic incident because I'm so distracting when I bend over to pick up a penny
criminal trespass
Crying too profusely & profoundly
cussing
Disturbing the Peace
Drawing on public spaces
Drinking out of Catholics holy water
Driving down one way streets
DUI
Erecting monuments
espousing anarchy
Falling asleep at a Red light
Farting in public
Female nipple exposure
Fist fighting locals
Guerilla art
honestly, I'm just not that cool
Honesty
I am not saying
illegal left turns
Primal screaming
irreverence towards the Spanish Colonial heritage
Jaywalking
Jaywalking while walking my dog
Loving Santa Fe too much.
None of above ....
None of the above!
Not giving myself enough time off
Performance art on the street without a license
personality
planting trees in parks without permission
protesting
public art
running into cars with Texas license plates
sarcasm
Sass
Saying Meowwolf is overrated.
shoplifting, indecent exposure, bank robbery, breaking and entering, possession of controlled substances, vandalizing monuments, toppling monuments, urinating on monuments, everything
shouting at the unmasked tourists
speeding
speeding?
Stealing posters
Stopping at a yellow light
That's too personal
trespassing
Trespassing
vandalizing monuments, toppling monuments, False accusations
well, not leaving dirty finger prints on this test
yelling at capitalists on the plaza
yelling at Texans

17

If YOU could choose a generation—other than the one you were born into—what would it be?

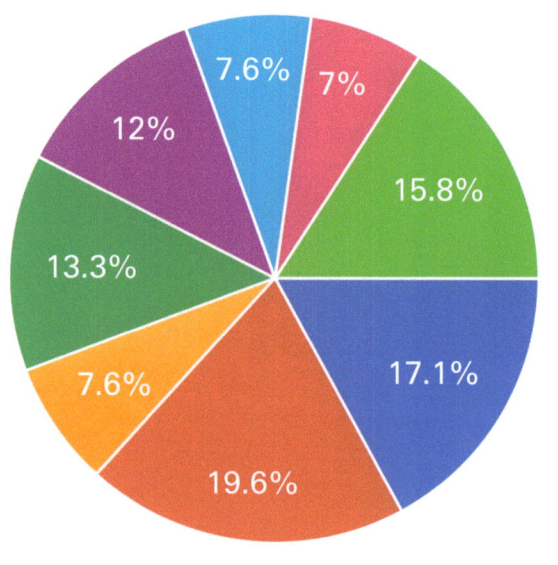

- Lost Generation (1883–1900)
- Greatest Generation (1901–1927)
- Silent Generation (1928–1945)
- Baby Boomers (1946–1964)
- Gen X (1965–1980)
- Millennials (1981–1996)
- Gen Z (1997–2012)
- Generation Alpha (2013–2022)

What defines us most as human?

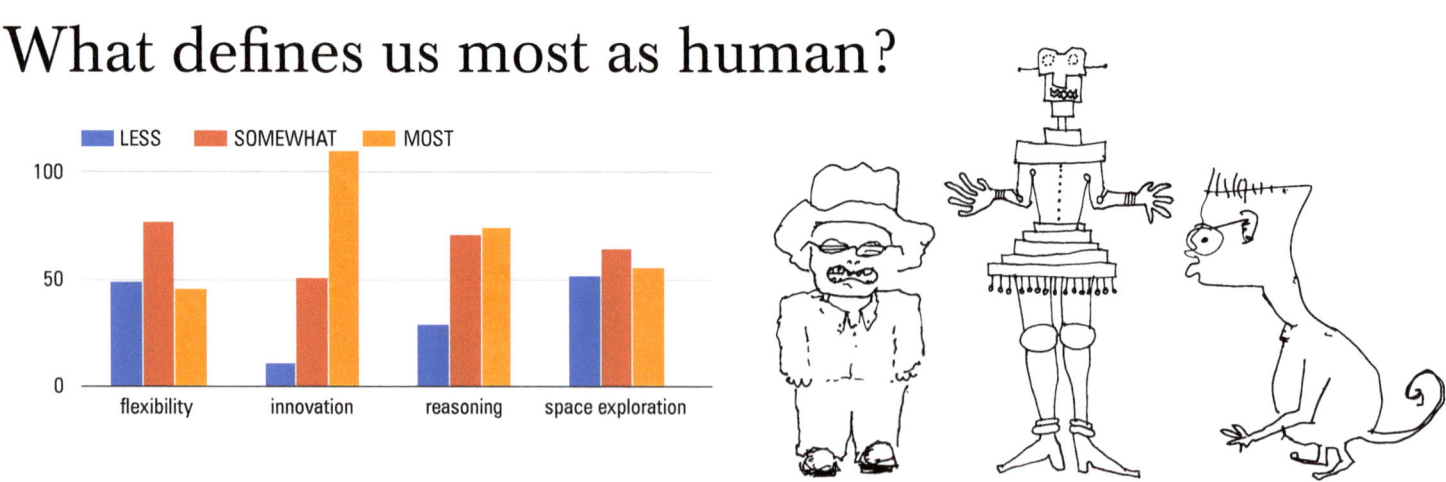

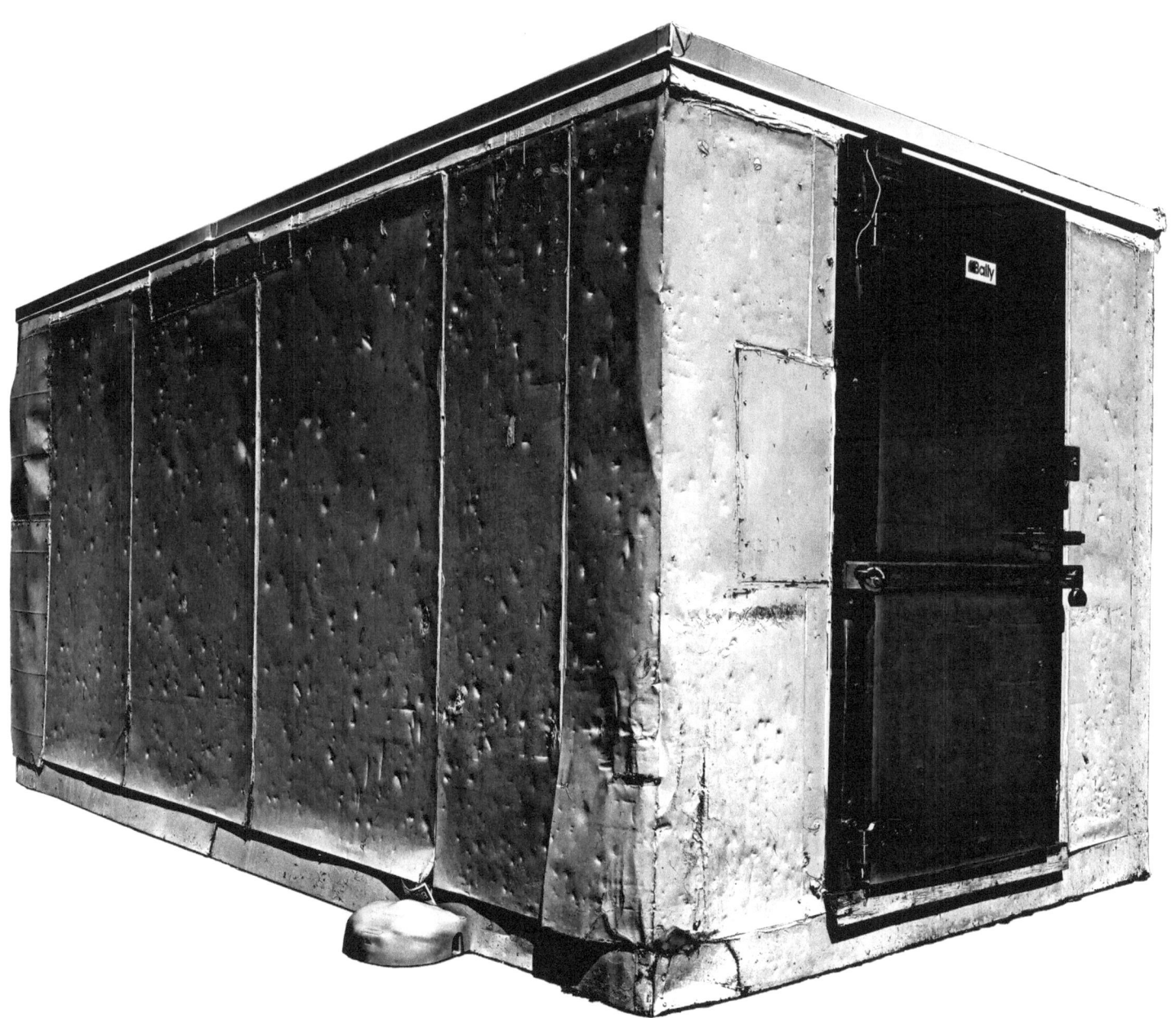

What is inside this box behind Trader Joe's shopping center in Santa Fe?

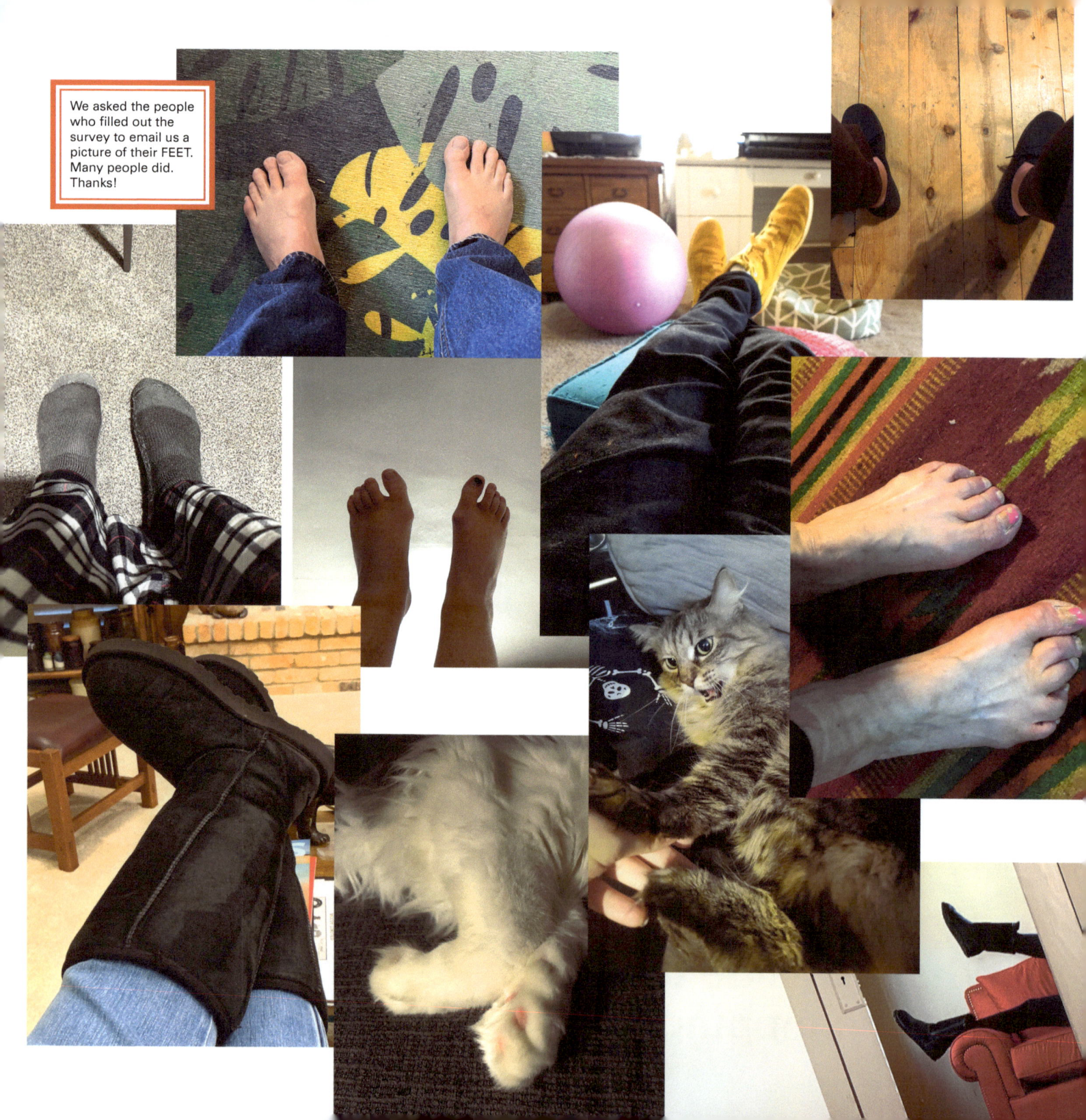

We asked the people who filled out the survey to email us a picture of their FEET. Many people did. Thanks!

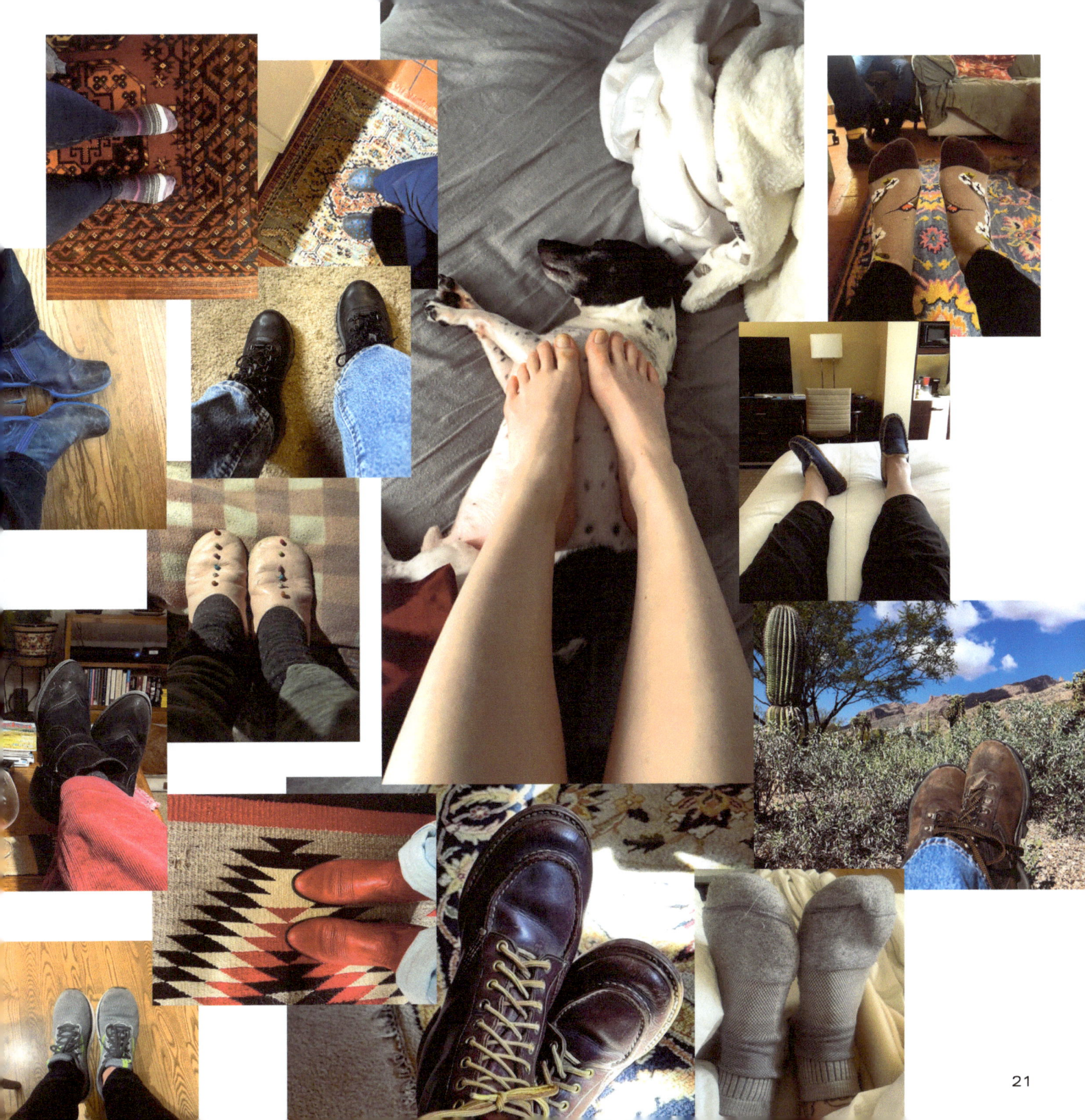

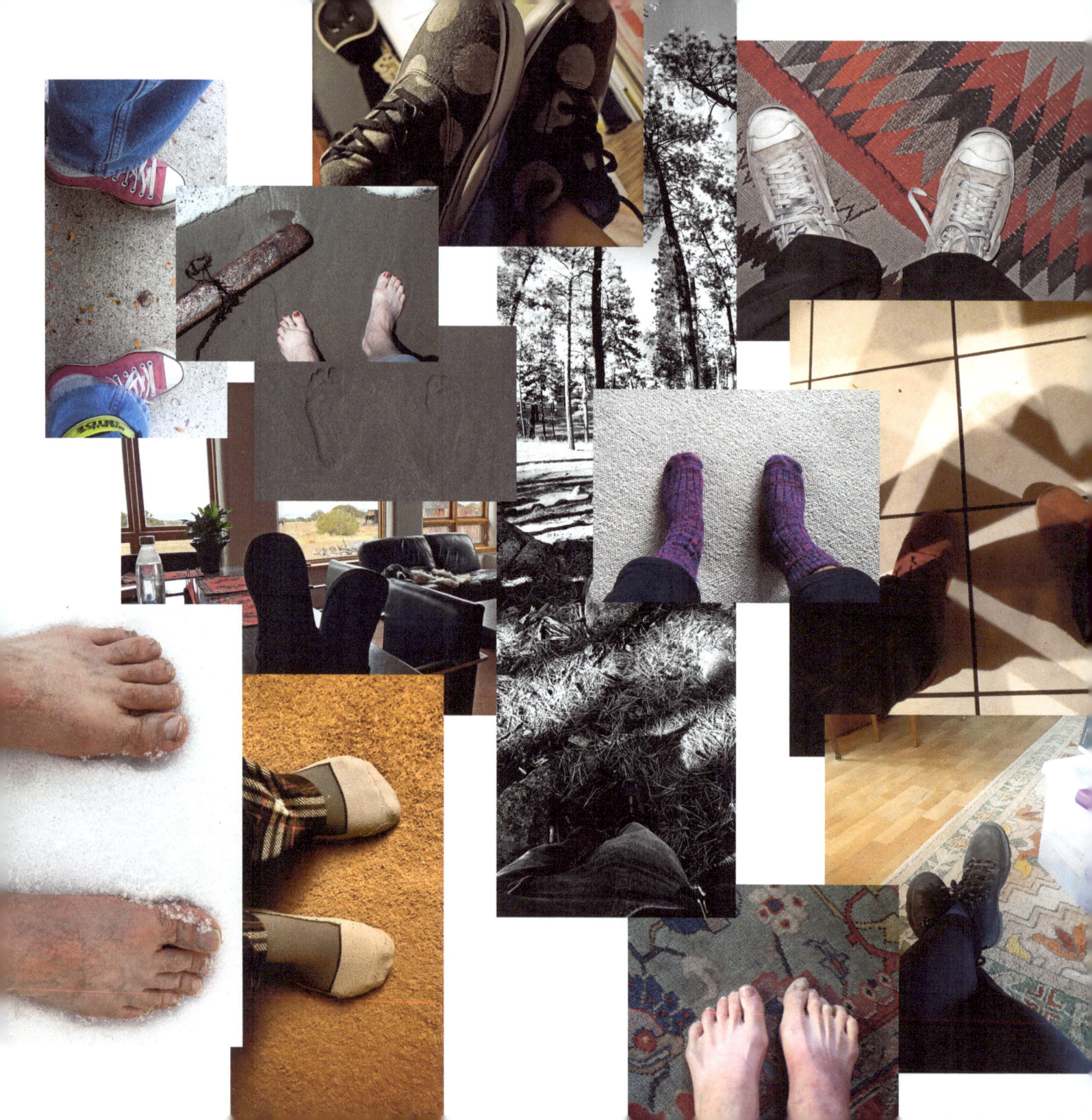

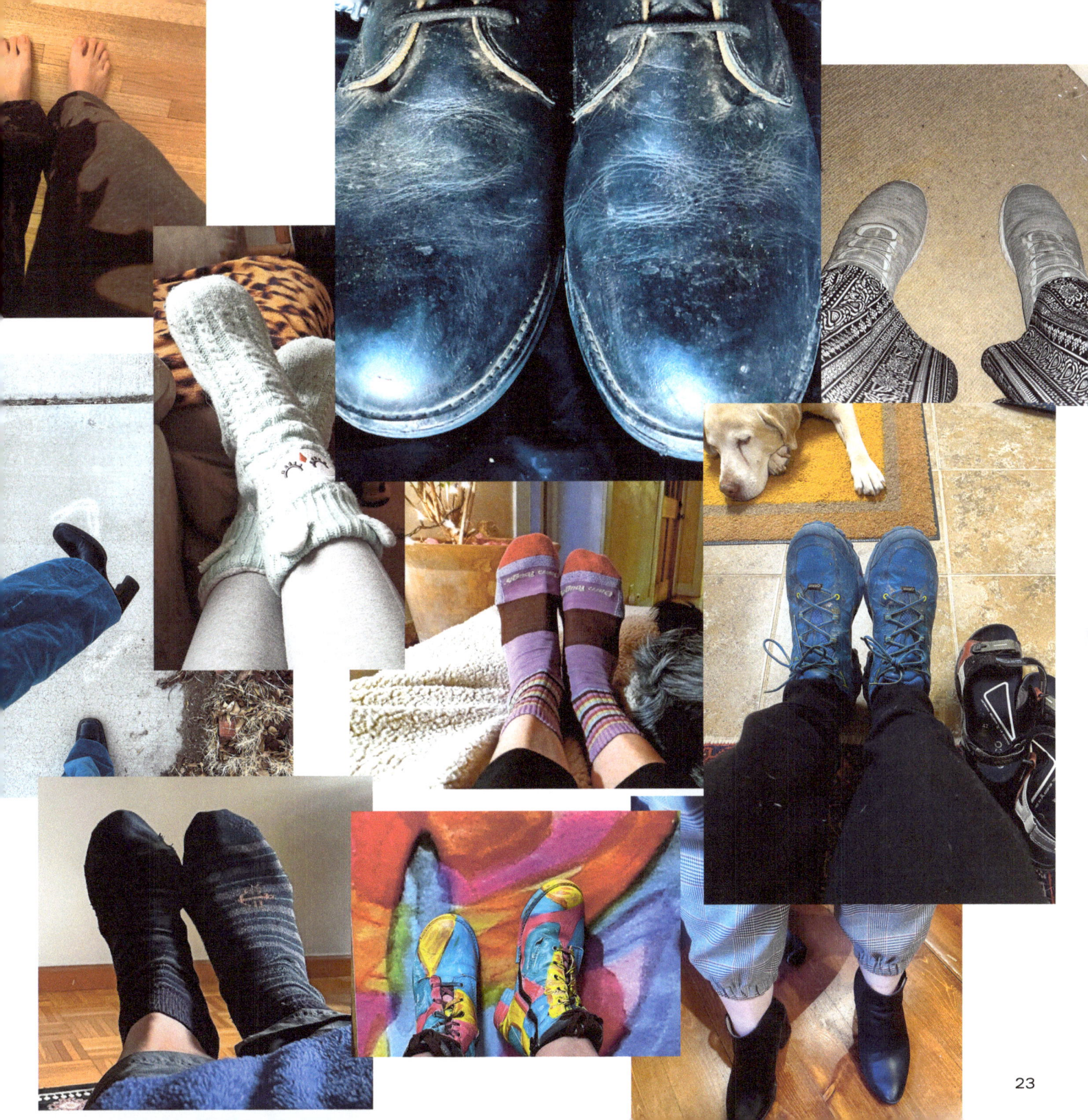

When are you evil?

11:30pm
11:34 AM
3 glasses in
3:15pm
5:00-5:15am
After 4 unnecessary "reply alls."
after dark
After too many SF nut brown ales
All the time
all the time
Am I evil I don't think so.
Around deadheads?
Around Republicans
as often as i can
At the ballot box
At the right times
backed in a corner
Before coffee
Before coffee and on full moons
complicity with whiteness
Depends on the mood.
depends who is judging me
Depends who's looking
Devious but not evil
Don't wake hungry mama bear.
driving
every other night
Gratefully not
Hmmm -- I don't think I'm evil ever. Except ... hmmm let me think about that. Maybe sometimes -- but don't want to think about it...but then again -- maybe sometimes when I don't realize it.
Hopefully never
i try not to be
In my dreams
in my head
in my mind
in my revenge fantasies.
In the face of injustice
January 6
just sometimes
late at night
Late at nihght
less now than when I was in my teens and 20's but probably most when I've been wronged.
Mad
Me? Never

Mondays and Thursdays
Moonshine or tequila that's why I had to quit
Most of the time, in part.
Needs work
Never [8 more times]
never :)
Never if I can help it.
Never, I believe
Not
Nothing is either good or bad but thinking makes it so
now
occasionally
often in other people's minds
On the second Tuesday of every week
only in speaking of possibilities
Only when you are, darling.
oooo, when i'm writing in my journal
... or maybe WHERE
Pulling weeds
Rarely but you never know
see bear/cougar question above
Situationally
Sleeping
Sometimes
The day before my moon, but only inside
Thursdays
Transiting from cerebral cortex and amygdaloid
unkind thoughts
When a student has done nothing all semester and suddenly wants to bring their grade up. It's evil how much I enjoy telling them they missed the deadlines.
When confronted by an angry bee. I am capable of murder. I hope.
when confronted with blatant bullish*t & assh*les
when cornered
When encountering laughing bears
When fences need knocking down
when I am in TJ Maxx
When I am overworked and feel drained. Plus when my subconscious says things that are really not OK
when I am sanguine about the death of anti-vaxxers
When I am thoughtless
when I am very bored
When I come across a misogynist
when i don't know and pretend i do
When I don't want to be

When I draw a major arcana on a tarot reading. I average 4 readings daily
When I drink too much and think I am funny
when I fail to acknowledge my shortcomings
When I have a submissive to play with
when I judge men I have never met based solely on their names. like, Seth is probably a bad dude, but I'm not even giving him a chance.
When I leave the rubber chicken under my partners pillow, so it makes a loud squeal when they sit on it
When I think of my ex husband
when I want to be
when I'm at my most passive aggressive
when i'm cursing my enemies
when i'm hungry
When I'm hungry, angry, lonely or tired: HALT
when i'm too focused on myself
When I'm inconvenienced and I forget my shared humanity with humanity.
When necessary
When no one is looking
When overlooking someone else playing Scrabble badly.
When people don't want to hear what's going on
When reading/ thinking about our past President.....
when someone hurts someone I care for
When someone is "whupping" a child in public.
When someone is evil to me
when someone takes my Dunkers.
when taking surveys
When the bears dance and steal your face
When the health care system fucks me
when the mood hits
when there's no time, someone's sick and coughing on me, i'm over-caffeinated, AND i've lost track of my will toward kindness, all on the same day!
When thinking about racists, mysogynists etc.
When wronged
When you treat people like things
Whenever it's convenient
While others are sleeping
Who? Sweet little me?
With stupid people

According to our survey
THERE IS NO

- **Free Lunch**   34.6%
- **Santa Claus**   35.8%
- **Silver Bullet**   34%
- or . . .

all of the above
all of the fucking above
all the above
american dream
American exceptionalism
Answer
Away
boogey man (or boogey woman) (or boogey LGBTQI)
Business like show business
business like show business
Caffeine-free Diet Coke
Common denominator
Common Sense
conspiracy
constant happiness
Democracy
easy answer
End to this survey.
escape
evil
Good cliché
Happy ever after all the time.
joy in Mudville
Justice without peace
motorcycles
place like home
Right answer
Sasquatch
Satisfaction, afterlife, second chance, going back
Second Tuesday in a week

Silver bullets exist in the literal sense, but there is no panacea for any of our ills, Santa Claus does not exist as a physically objective living entity, but is based on a number of historical and mythical figures and holds a very real place in the imaginations and culture of quite a few people. While people use "there's no such thing as a free lunch" as a condescending "pull yourself up by your bootstraps" cliche, free lunches exist and we have the ability and moral responsibility to provide them to all who need them.

Sky Fairy
Something
Stinking badges
such thing as, 'a virus gives a damn about my opinion about it.'
Surrender!
The silver bullet is for Santa Claus. Or it would be, if either existed
There, there
Time and Space
Time like the present
True religion
Truth without recognizing the participation of one's unconscious in every day.
vegan yeast
way I'm letting you leave without a hug
way out
Way out of climate change until human stop reproducing at such a rapid rate.
Way out of this
widespread voter fraud
Winning lottery ticket, knight on a white horse
WMD

WHAT do you think was the most over-used word in 2021?

fungible (12.8%)
identity (4.9%)
socialism (9.8%)
conversation (0.6%)
meta-anything (31.7%)

WHAT do you *think*

2020	fucking covid	PIVOT	Anti- (fill in space)	COVID	Divided
amazing	Gratitude	post-covid		COVID	downturn
anxiety	I	Quarantine	apocalypse or boring or covid	Covid	Emotional damage
bespoke	? I dont think words are overused	Rigged		COVID	Encaustic
business accelerator startup launchpad	Inflation	Robust	Art	covid	Endemic
cancel	Jab	Sausage-making	before	Covid	endemic
community, diversity	Lean-in	Simp	bespoke OR woke	covid	Evangelical
conversation	literally (used figuratively)	spirituality		Covid	failed
covid	Mask	Stolen	Bet	covid	fake news
covid	meme	Story-telling	Brandon	Covid	fascism
COVID	New normal	They, Them, Theirs	Brandon	COVID	figuratively (used literally)
covid	no	Trump	Bubble	Covid	
covid	Normal	trump	bungle	Covid!!!	
covid	overreach	Twenty	cancel	Cringe	filibuster
covid	pandemic	Uncertain	catastrophic	Crypto	Fire
Covid	pandemic	unprecedented	collapse	Curated	Fragmented
COVID-19	pandemic	unprecedented	Compliance	Deep dive	Free
Covid!!!	pandemic	Unprecedented	Conspiracy	Democracy	Freedom
Curated	pandemic	Unprecedented	Covid	disrupt	
curated	Pandemic	Unprecedented			
either "the" or "a".	patroit	Unprecedented			
Free	pivot	Vaccinate			

will be the most over-used word in 2022?

freedom
fuck
Fungible
Fungible
Gender
Heaven only knows!
Hope
hope
Hopefully — recovered
hoping it's "relief"
I
? I dont think words are overused
I, Me, Mine
Idk
Inflation

Jab
Joe Manchin or Kyrsten Sinema
Kerplunk
Liars
Mandate
Mask-up
material
Me
meme
Meta
Meta
Meta
Meta-something
meta-anything
meta-anything
metastasy

Metaverse
metaverse
Mid-term Elections
midterms
new normal
new normal
New-normal
NFT
Nfts
no
No se.
Normal
Normal
Normal
nothingburger
Omicrom
omicron
Omicron

Omicron
other
Oy Vey
pandemic
pandemic
Pandemic
pandemic
Pandemic
Patriot
persnickety
Pivot
PIVOT
polarization
Poly amorous
post-covid
post-pandemic
post-pandemic
probably
Regenerative

Rigged
Scabrous
shitshow
Simp
Somatic
space -- as in, he's been working in that space for most of his career
Still meta-anything
Supposedly testing
The or and.
tired
trump
Trump
Twenty

Twenty twenty-two
Uncertain
unprecedented
unprecedented
Vaccine
vaccine
vaccine
virtual
Whatever they call the NEXT strain of Corona virus
Why
Wildfire
WTF
yass

27

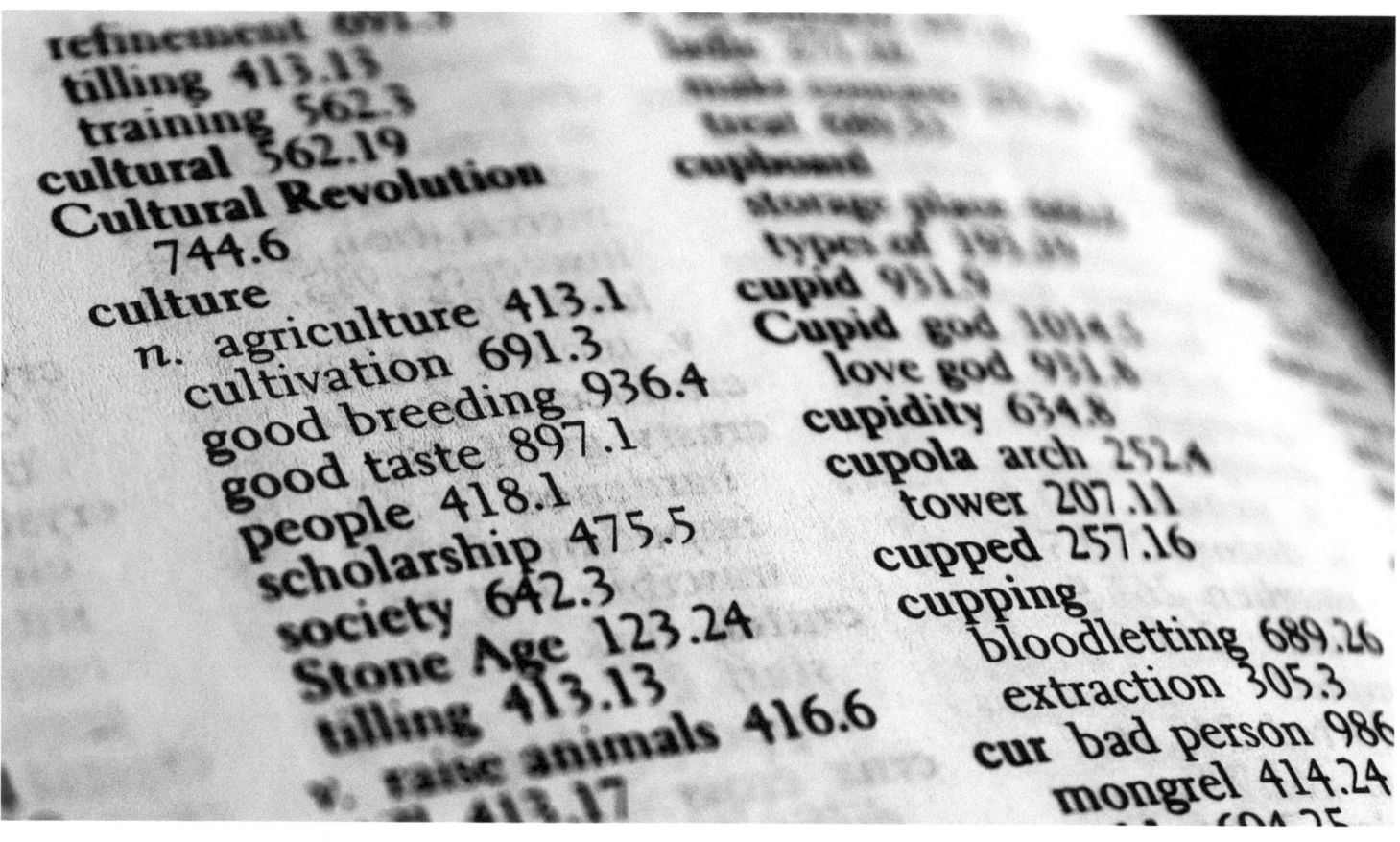

WHAT DOES "CULTURE" MEAN TO YOU?

A beautiful expression of humanity

a collection of stories a group of people tell themselves

a hairdo

A look beyond one's immediate sphere.

A place to belong

A set of pre-programmed ideals that provide a bubble from which we experience the world

a small amount of thought or bacteria which given the proper conditions can expand and influence surrounding organisms.

A society where art/music/theatre/literature are available to all people starting from birth.

A tangy food item

A way of life

Access to the arts for all.

agreed-upon norms

all that keeps me in the lines, safely

An aggregate group expression of groupness, meaning a shared set of (implicit and explicit) values, ideas, concepts, and rules of behavior that allow a social group to function and perpetuate itself.

an agreed upon set of rituals and attitudes that respond to circumstances of a specific time that is immediately in the past.

An excuse to discriminate

Appreciation of the arts

Art, food, traditions

art, togetherness

Arts and social institutions of a certain area

bacteria

behavior and things created in your society

beliefs, traditions, and values of groups of people shaped by family, society, history, geography. Things that grow in a petri dish.

Black stylist attire

Celebration of traditions from specific groups of people.

Cheese

Collective knowledge and shared practices of a group of people

collective mores

Collective wisdom, ritual, language, and creativity—often goes unacknowledged.

community

Connection through creativity

culture is an expression of reality and society and individual and collective experiences that are rooted in specific places and peoples

Culture is rarely mean to me

culture to me is simply the aggregate of what people do, alone and in groups.

Customs, art, social flavor. Or growing fun thing in petri dishes.

Customs, practices, and art of a specific area

Da whole schmear

Deep history

Depends on the context

Diversity, Artistic, Community

enriched, refined and supported human activities either endemic to a region or globally respected as a specific and developed training which results in art.

Everything

fascinating development of humans

Focused energy

Food choices!

food, language, dance, music, literature, story telling, where you think the gods live

freedom

Good and such

Green Chile

Having identity

How individuals/groups/organizations define themselves through art, music, language, religion and interactions

Human residue

Human respect and cooperation with nonhuman nature

humanity

identity

Inherited sense of belonging and how it's expressed through customs like art, music, and food

It is ever changing

It's kinda anthropological.

la gente! art!!! everything that people make becomes part of the culture and makes it up, whether it's traditions or art or stories…. it's all about what people make

Life

Lifeways

Lots of good thoughts

manipulation

Milk. Definitely milk.

Mind broadening

Money.

More antibiotics

More than food, shelter or clothing.

music, rituals, food, shared values, shared experiences

myths and symbols shared by a certain group

not much

not raw

nuff said

Oh lordy, art and music and stuff like that. hate that word.

ooh i choose cultured pearl - it means that what is asymmetrical can be beautiful :)

Opportunity

Ordering Chocolate milk and grilled cheese at a fancy restaurant.

passing on traditions that are inclusive and life-affirming

past into present

Penicillin.

Recognition and integration of The Arts, History and Science

Respect for the past and history. Strive to create experiences in the arts for the future.

Self-determination

Shared behavior, customs, food, traditions, stories, ways of living and being

Shared values, history, traditions, and outlook

social behaviors and norms of a certain society including art, laws, customs, etc.

Something with no ""practical"" value that we can't live without.

Sometimes oppression, other times inspiration, and in between, mediocrity.

Stuff people do

The ability to communicate in a specific way.

The air we breathe, the water we swim in, the soup we eat, the stories we tell all blended up.

The arts and dreams of the collective

The arts, traditions and customs, social ways of life within a group of people, their achievements, lifestyles, habits and values morally, their religions and beliefs within the society a group of people belong. It is passed on from generation to generation so it is learned.

The broad nature of the mores, traditions, art and beauty of our surroundings.

The celebration of the scared things that fortified my ancestors.

The collection of habits, actions, creations that make life enjoyable

the germinated texture of community

The immaterial thing that makes up our lives.

the intersection of art and tradition

The shared or collective products of thinking and making of a group.

The sum total of human life experiences

The thing that makes you weird to other people when you leave home but you can't see it and neither can your mom

the unique values, foods, dance, art, music, acceptable behaviors of members of a community

"The way we do things around here" -Brene Brown

The way we live

the wonderful things humans do together

thinking and kindness

tradition + expression

Tradition from someone's background and/or family

Traditions and artifacts and beliefs and creativity of a community

traditions passed down

traditions that build a social structure

Traditions through which we form bonds with others.

traits shared by others, something that has an effect over what a group of people act or do

vaginal yeast infections

We love in a society (autocorrect, but I'm keeping it, meant to be)

what is around you

what your people do

Whatever it is we are losing it

Wow that's quite a question to answer in a tiny space

Writing our own stories

yogurt

Yogurts, kefir

"THE NEXT BIG THING"
(according to our survey participants)

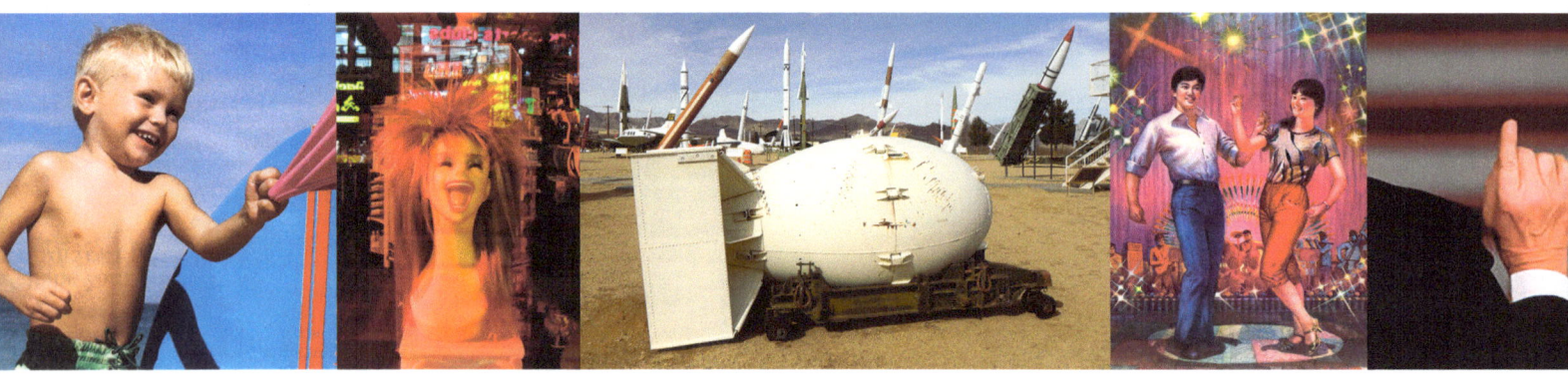

A US dictatorship

A virus

AI Robots doing everything rendering human beings only good for making art and conversation

All of the above

Americans killing americans in defense of america

annihilation

Another COVID varient

another strain of covid, probably :/

AR and VR and I'm creating content now

Armageddon

Art that makes fun of western art

avocado toast

Big hair

Brick and mortar stores — small scale

Broccoli

Burst of the bitcoin bubble

Caitlyn Jenner gets GOP endorsement for 2024 presidential election

Cave Dwelling

cbd chocolate bananas on a stick

Clearly the extinction of the huida kiddush.

Climate change protection communities for billionaires

Climate Collapse

climate correction

Climate refugees

common sense

Compost

Corn pudding

COVID parties

Dance parties in the metaverse.

dancing

dancing

Death

depends on what 'group' you belong to

Despair

Dictatorship

Disposable designer clothing, shoes, hats, goggles, face shields, gloves and mittens. One person portable bars.

Don't look up ... :)

don't really care

Dropping out of high school

Dual gender for everyone

Earwax

Economic slowdown

Facism.

fingerless gloves

Flying car

Flying cars

Flying cars

Flying Space Cars

Folks getting off of social media and giving up cell phones.

Fun natural fun

Gathering again???

Going out with a bang

Going to Mars

Hairy drag queens.

Hiding from the natural disasters we have created

High tech disguised as low tech

Hopefully not civil war

Houses built out of recycled plastic

How little privacy we have

Human resource credits

I feel like pudding is due for a comeback…

I'm sad that it's probably some kind of robot

I'm too tired to think of anything

Incrementalism

Inner peace

Jellies. We've seen most of the other mid-nineties fashion come back, so why not Jellies?

Kindness

kindness and compassion

Kindnesses

Lettuce

little -- small is beautiful -- save the planet

Love

Love

Making it illegal for kids to be on social media. I wish.

Marjorie Taylor Greene.

martyrs

mass migration to the north

me

Me

Me, hopefully.

Mending

More UFOs being identified

Mountains are big

Mouth vacuum

My exhibition in Santa Fe

My headache

Nebraska

New ways of reconciling our lizard brains with a post-capitalist hell-scape.

Nights on the town

nothingness, the lack of anything

omega

Omicron (sadly)

Our meta verse world.

parties

penmanship

People in gas masks

Peptides

pocket-sized disco balls filled with ketamine

Pokémon STAY

Race to clean carbon from atmosphere

Recycled air helmets

Reliquary of the Olympian Gods

Removing our masks

Revolution

Robot teachers

Salt

Sand colonics.

small things

Some kinda meme

some- thing small

Soylent green

Space tourism

Space travel

Srt

Stop

Suicide parties

sunset

that gum you like

the bomb

The bomb

The death of Trump

The fall of Rome 2

three day work weeks

Time

Trust

trying to find/grow food, once the climate change screws us all

Universal healthcare.

Virtual Art Viewing

Water

We will return to our roots of civility, generosity, kindness and love, leaving behind anger, hostility, murdering and anxiety.

Whatever comes next

Whatever it is, I hope it comes with a side of chile!

wigs + smiles, a community brunch

Words spontaneously combust mid-articulation.

world war 3. i wish i were kidding

World War III -- I hope not!

Writing left handed

Your show

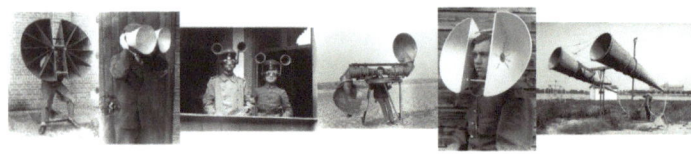

WHAT TYPE OF "SURVEY" DO YOU PREFER?

- one that promotes illogical thinking and impulsiveness (11.5%)
- one that improves efficiency of mentation and perception (10.3%)
- one that renders the induction of hypnosis easier and more effective (4.8%)
- one that enhances the ability of an individual to resist brainwashing (26.1%)
- one that lowers individual ambition and encourages induction into a group (2.4%)
- one that produces pure euphoria with no subsequent letdown (29.7%)

OTHER:

An honest one

And how

brief ones

Increase in knowledge

One for which I know the answers and they are quick to answer (hint hint)

one in which 'not knowing' is just fine

one that allows for infinite "why's?"

one that creates the revelation that we (all species) are relatives

One that doesn't ask questions.

One that improves the efficiency of menstruation and perspiration

one that induces playfulness and experimentation

one that is amusing

One that is carried out by British detectives in a crime drama on TV

one that pays $30k

One that slows my metabolism

one that subliminally reprograms my sense of place

one that watches to see what happens

one with answers

open-minded curiosity

outquiry

Raising joy.

Scientific

Something daring, full of danger and uncertainty.

stimulating and brief

WHAT IS A "JACKALOPE"?

A jack-o'-lantern carved from a cantaloupe 7.2%
A jack-in-the-box with a jump rope 2.8%
A portmanteau of a jackrabbit and an antelope 77.3%
A mercado on Cerrillos Road in Santa Fe 29.8%

"OTHER" answers included:

a rare animal

a ghost of what once was

A guy in a slow spacious run while self stimulating

A jackass and a misspelled dope

a joke on tourists

a long earred fictiohopping

a rabbit with antlers

A style of cowboy running while holding a bottle of Jack Daniels

A textile store located in cerillos rd. A home to prairie dogs.

a very shy, rare, biologically impossible cross-bred animal, last sited near Quemado, NM.

an flea market on cerilous

An infamous cryptid

I saw one or three specimens at the university of Zurich a few years back, Einstein attended. I have a couple of pictures of them on display there, rabbits with small antlers.

I was told once, but I forget

Jack "hit the road" and was then wed without telling his family.

Jackalope is the running gait of a jackel... duh.

Man of odd gait

My spirit animal!

NM long distance runners who delivered mail over mountains and prairies

Offspring of a jack rabbit and an antelope

Postcard Celebrity

Real

the sound of my brain taking this inquiry (bravo)

The way Jack wants to get married?

The young woman that ran off with Jack to get married

Two grooms named Jack eloping

When a woman runs off to marry a man named Jack.

when Captain Sparrow strolls in a slightly drunken yet sexy fashion down the deck

A FEW FACTS INCLUDED IN THE SURVEY

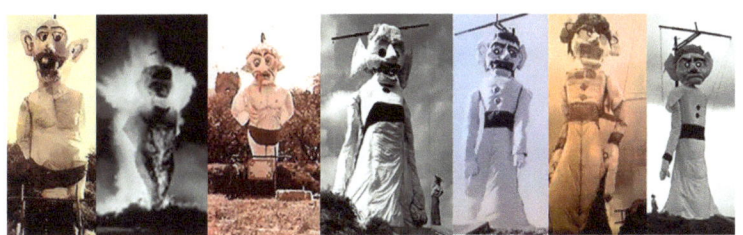

Zozobra was first burned at a private party in artist Will Shuster's backyard in 1924. He and his friends thought it would be fun to build a big marionette, drink a lot of tequila, and set the thing on fire. Of course everybody in town heard about it. The next year they all showed up. It was such a success that the City of Santa Fe took over in 1926 and has been making and burning bigger and better marionettes ever since. Old Man Gloom is 50 feet tall now and over 60,000 people show up and go crazy. Everyone is invited to voice their "gloom" on slips of paper, which are then burned up inside Zozobra.

Pueblo lands, **Oga Po'geh** in Tewa (or "White Shell Water Place"), were named **La Villa Real de la Santa Fe de San Francisco de Asis** by Spanish settlers, and designated a territory in 1610. In 1680, Pueblo peoples revolted, inspired by the Tewa religious leader Po'pay. The revolt was successful, causing the colonists to retreat. Twelve years later, the territory was recaptured by Don Diego de Vargas after a bloody battle. Angered by the resistance, de Vargas executed 70 Pueblo elders on the Santa Fe Plaza. A statue of de Vargas was recently removed from Cathedral Park. "DeVargas Center" currently names the shopping mall on Guadalupe Street.

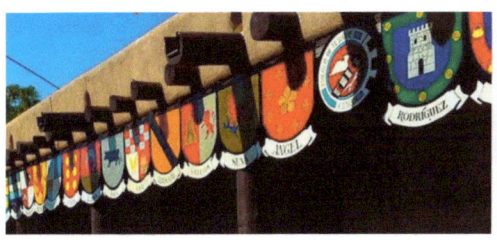 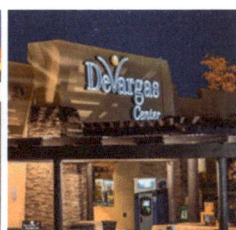

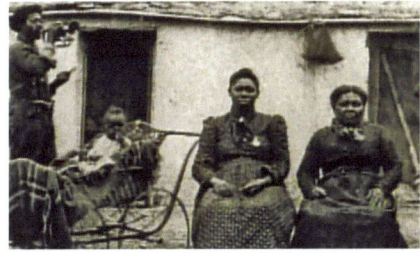

Blackdom, New Mexico, was a freedom colony of all-Black homesteaders, founded in 1901 by Frank Boyer and family. He was a teacher from Georgia fleeing the KKK. He dug a well and began farming 18 miles SW of Roswell, after travelling on foot over a thousand miles to land he'd heard of from his father, who'd fought there in the Mexican-American War. Incorporated in 1903 by 13 people, Blackdom grew to several hundred residents, with a newspaper, hotel, school, Post Office, and an annual Juneteenth celebration. After a series of droughts and decline in crop prices, it was largely deserted by the mid-1920s, but it had succeeded for more than two decades as an independent society.

The **Manhattan Project** hired Dorothy McKibbin in 1943 to run its administrative hub located in Sena Plaza across the street from St. Francis Cathedral. She greeted workers and their families as they arrived on the train from Lamy, completing their paperwork before they went on to Los Alamos, "The Hill." A close friend to Oppenheimer, she was indispensable to the project and subsequently named a "Living Treasure of Santa Fe." Sena Plaza was originally constructed in the 1600s, extended into a 33-room hacienda in the late 1800s, and now houses shops and restaurants.

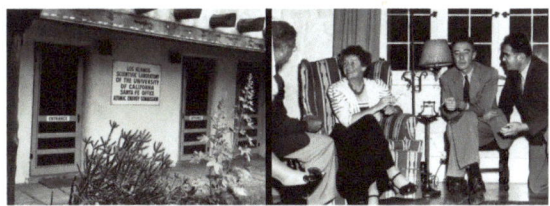

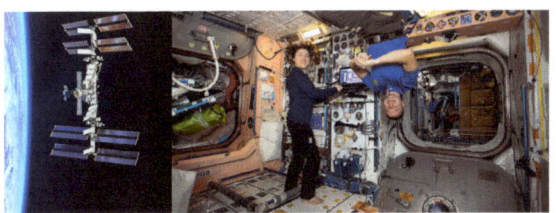

Hatch chile pepper seeds from New Mexico arrived on June 2021 at the International Space Station aboard SpaceX's 22nd resupply mission as part of NASA's Plant Habitat experiments. If successful, this crop will be added to the astronaut's diet. In space, crew members often lose a sense of taste and smell and so prefer spicy foods. Peppers are also high in Vitamin C and other nutrients. Researchers spent 2 years evaluating dozens of peppers before selecting the NuMex Española Improved variety, saying this pepper "had all the makings of a viable space crop."

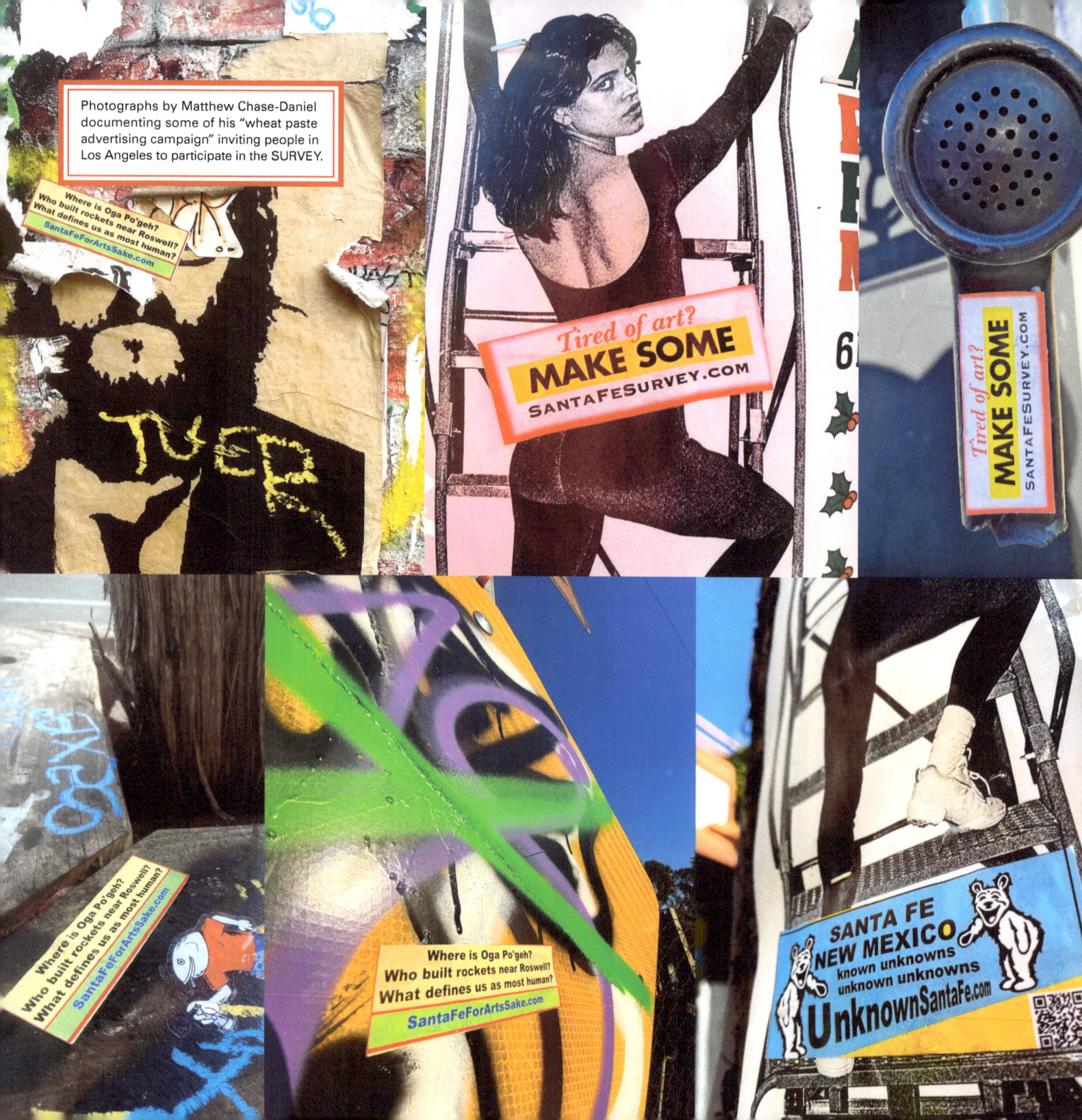

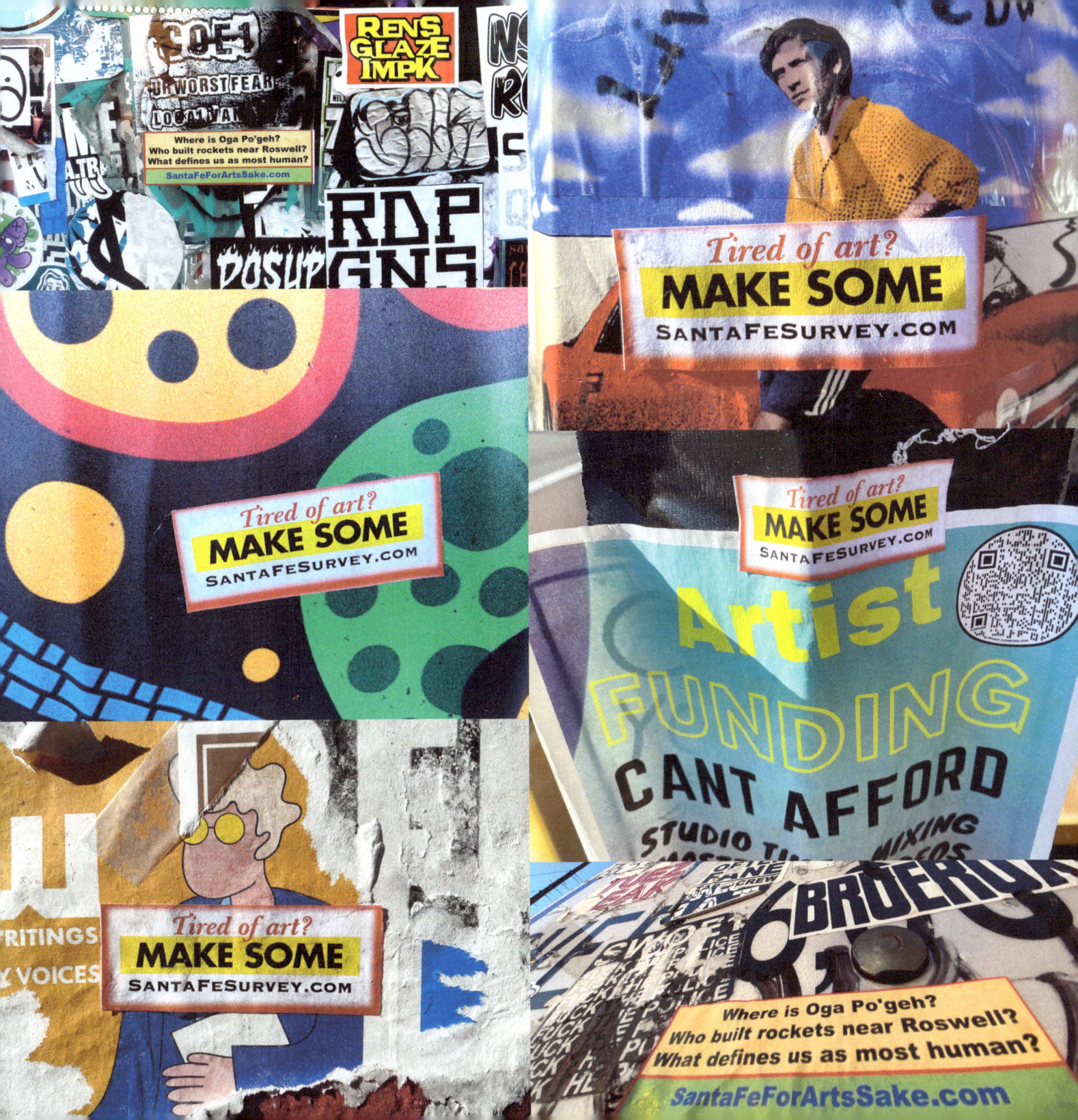

PAGES 36–39: Selected questions and responses from the first online survey, **Why is art like an alligator?**, created by Burning Books for Axle Contemporary as part of CURRENTS New Media 2021.

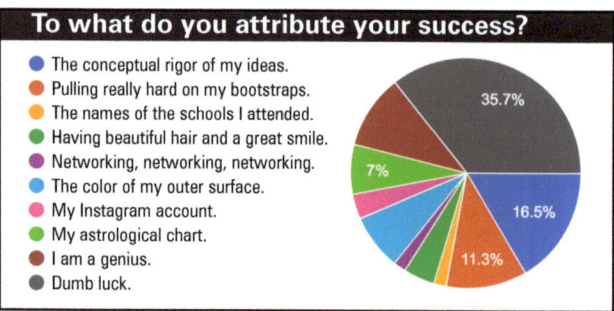

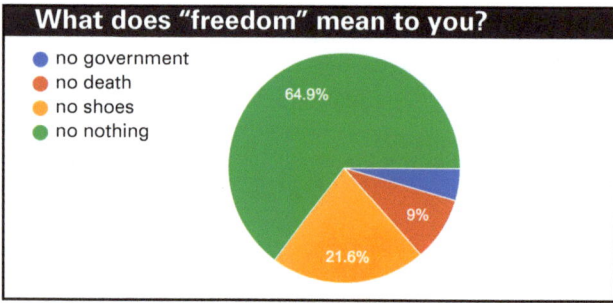

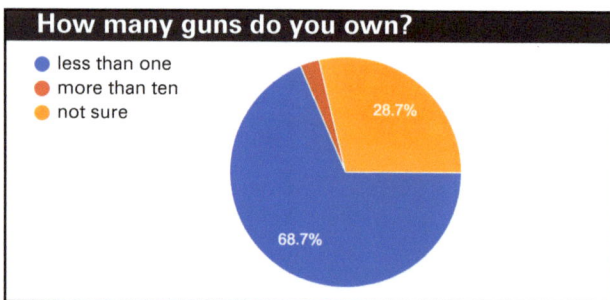

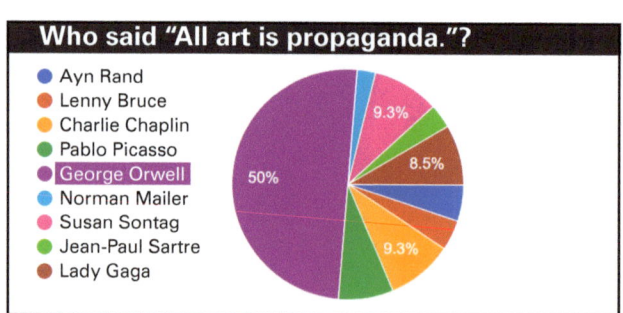

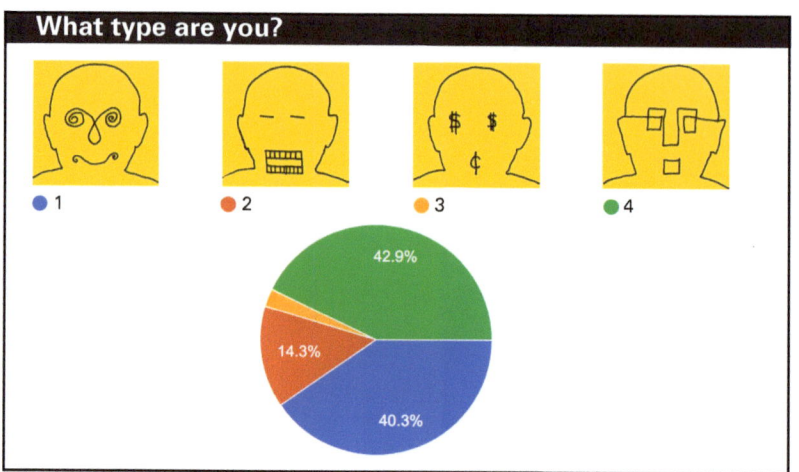

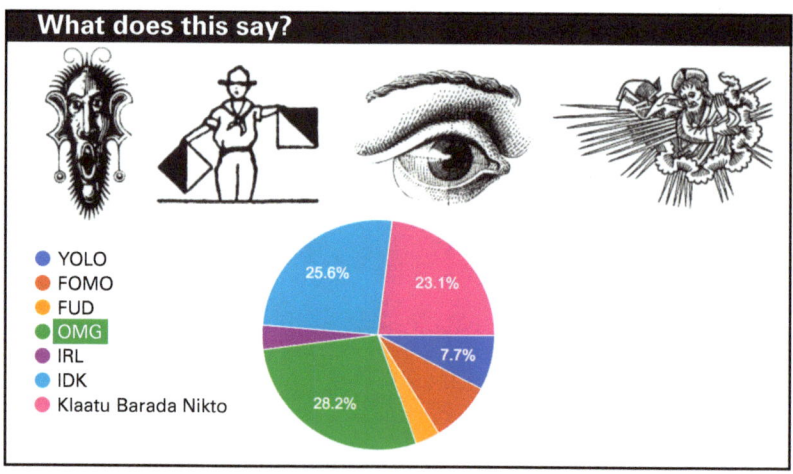

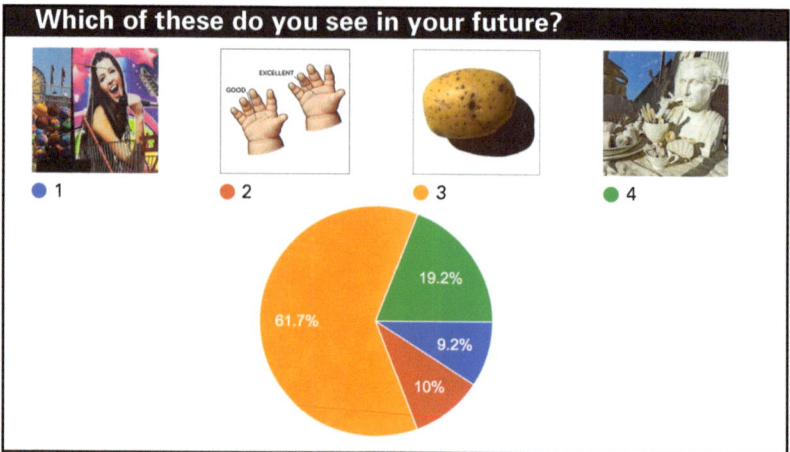

36

How many stop signs can you find in this picture?

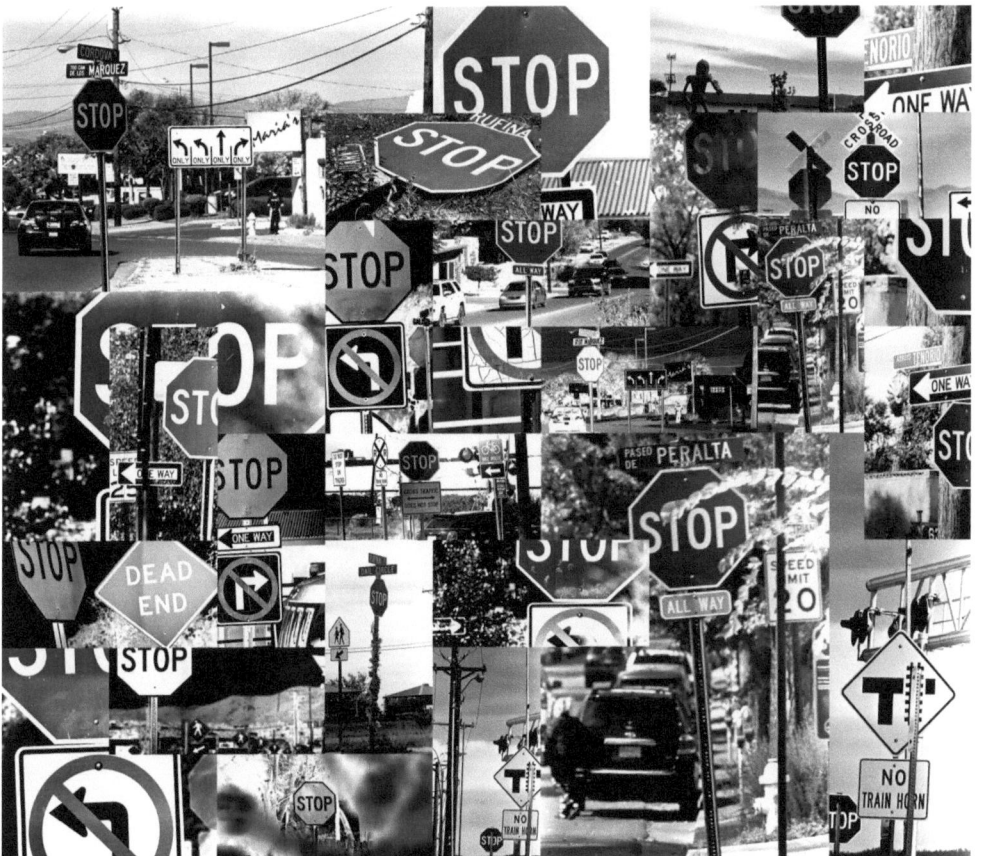

<%>	16	22	25	26	Thirty	Lots
one	17	22	25	26	31 + the infinitude of stop signs in our own minds, maaaan	Lots
One	18	22	25	26		lots
One	18	22 and 4 halves.	25	26 maybe - I don't like counting things	31 I am not a robot.	lots of them
1	18	23	LOL :-) 25 but that was one pass of counting so I'd guess there are a few more than that. I'm mostly enjoying the effect of all of them collaged together!	27	36	Many
3	18	23		27	37	many
no <3	19	23		27	37	many
4	19.5	23		at least 27	42	More than enough
Eleventeen	20	23 (And I am not a robot!)		27ish	45	more than I am willing to count
eleventy twoty forty	20			[correct answer is 28]	100	More than I want to count
12	21	24		29	333	More than needed
12	21	24	26	29	3000	multiplicity
15	21	24	26	30	69420	None
15 or so	21	25	26		69420	Not interested in knowing
					8,753	Several
					a lot	Signs of what?
					A lot	so many
					A lot	some among others
					a lot	There is only one stop sign
					a whole bunch.	There's no way I'm going to complete this task - I'm not your monkey
					All of them	
					all of them	
					almost all of them	too many
					are there any?	Too many
					brain hurt... <exiting visual cortex> <reboot soft>	Too many to try and count.
					Enough.	Too many to waste time counting them
					enuf	Too many.
					fuck off	who cares?
					I hate these things; they favor visual acuity.	why is a mouse when its spinning
					I only see pots	
					Infinity +1	

What is the strangest thing you actually believe?

A variation of simulation theory

ants are smarter than we are

art

astral travel

belief is just relief spelled with an upsidedown one-legged R

Birds talk to me

Birds talk to me

Creativity

Creativity

dick cdick chaney and donald trump have the same father

Energy

everything happens for a reason

fate

goodness will prevail

how can humans look into the past and see such naiveté, but then look at the present & future with such arrogance?

humanity is not entirely irredeemable

humans are animals

I am accompanied ethereally by six dragons in highly saturated hues.

I believe that relativity applies to each and every one of us.

I can really fly.

I don't believe anything strange

I exist

I exist outside of my physical body

I have a soul

I have magical powers

I have no strange beliefs, only transcendental ones.

i stop watches

I talk to dead people

I'm amongst enemies

I'm not really that old.

I'm worthless

if I knew I would stop believing it

In energy manifesting between people

It's all going to be ok

karma

lakes are persons

life has meaning

Mares.

Mind over matter.

Mind over matter.

my eyes change color

My father was reincarnated into a seal.

myself

Myself

N.A.

Not strange, no one is unique. We are all similar

Not sure.

one day there will be no violence

prayer, but only 1 prayer

Quantum entanglement

ranked choice voting is a good idea

Reincarnation

Robin Williams was just trying to cum

Santa Claus

Santa Claus

Science and God are both real.

Several politicians

Shapeshifting

Someday I will get to live by the ocean in an vital community

Someone will come to help

stones have souls

Tat tvam asi

That all life is interconnected to the extent that we share a universal subconscious

That all people are good

that anything is worthwhile

That Donald Trump is human.

That glowing health is dependent on consumption of copious quantities of butter

that hard work and best intentions pay off

That I am conscious

That I matter

That I will die and be forever dead

That I'm still here

that it's worth it

that my answer will actually make a difference

That my mustache is like Samson's hair

that my twin brother and I could communicate telepathically as children

That none of the things I believe are strange

That people actually don't like me

That the universe was designed with me in mind

That there are ghosts, and that they are good.

That there is a library in the time space continuum that contains the thoughts and experiences of every sentient being. Akashic Records!!!

That there is an unseen entity that creates each being

That there is hope

That there is no such thing as Randomness

That twiddling my thumbs helps me remain calm

That we are all connected

that we can all live peacefully together

that we can talk with the dead

That we've ALL been here before

the earth is round

The first and last words of a book tells story. Same as the sentence first and last. Why? Because that in stone those words and Waze people see the whole middle differently than each other.

The hereafter is a comfort but I don't believe it.

The imagination is a network of galatic portals

the infinite parallel universe thing

The most important things are all invisible

The truth.

The value of narrative construction

theocratic anarchism

There are things in the same place as us we don't see or know about and they probably didn't have a clue about us either.

There is beauty in everything.

there is spiritual connection between people before and after death

There will be a future that is not dystopian

This survey

ur mum

WALKING BAREFOOT IN GRASS FOR ELECTRIC BALANCE

We are between worlds

We are so tiny, in the scope of the universe, that our minds can't even comprehend how small we are.

We can get through this.

We live in our own simulations

we're not alone in the universe

Well that depends on who you ask!

Woop.

When did things go wrong?

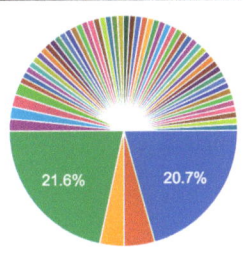

- When money was invented.
- When art schools were invented.
- When art fairs were invented.
- When the artist's statement was invented.
- Other:

Abrahamism
Agriculture
All of the above
Art critiques
Birth
Clickbait surveys in artsy language to hide the true intent
Day 2
Gunpowder.
I don't feel qualified to answer this (compared to my extreme qualifications in dirt estimation, for example)
In the beginning
industrial revolution
is something wrong?
It was clearly wrong when it all began
Light bulb, telephone, automobile, television, atomic bomb, it is all downhill.
Mesopotamian agricultural revolution
Not sure.
Nothing is wrong.
Nothing is wrong.
the big bang
They keep going right and wrong simultaneously
Things have gone exactly as they were supposed to, unfortunately.
Things haven't gone wrong.
this is a cute survey but reflexive anti-art world propaganda is boring
Wait, things are going wrong?
when agriculture was invented
when agriculture was invented
When agriculture was invented.
When art became a thing and not a process
When art was separated from life
When art wasn't re-invented.
When evolution forgot a key hominid survival attribute.
when government was invented
when greed and hate were invented
When he tried to push it just a little bit further
When humans arrived
When I forgot my keys.
When I was born
When I was born
when invention was invented
When invention was monetized for artist's statements, to be fair
When minding the store started
When people got jealous of artists.
When people started believing the artist's statement said something.
When questions were invented.
When race was invented
When religion was invented.
when the concept of self was invented
When the concept of wrong was invented
When the OJ Simpson/Kardashian reality TV was started.
When the roaring 20s ended.
When there became too many humans
when they created Patriarchy, duh
When we climbed down from the trees.
When we kept repeating our mistakes
when we started to commodify art
Whenever
Whenever
yes.

Have you ever paid attention to bollards?

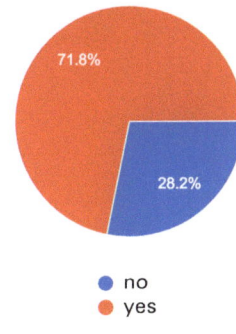

- no
- yes

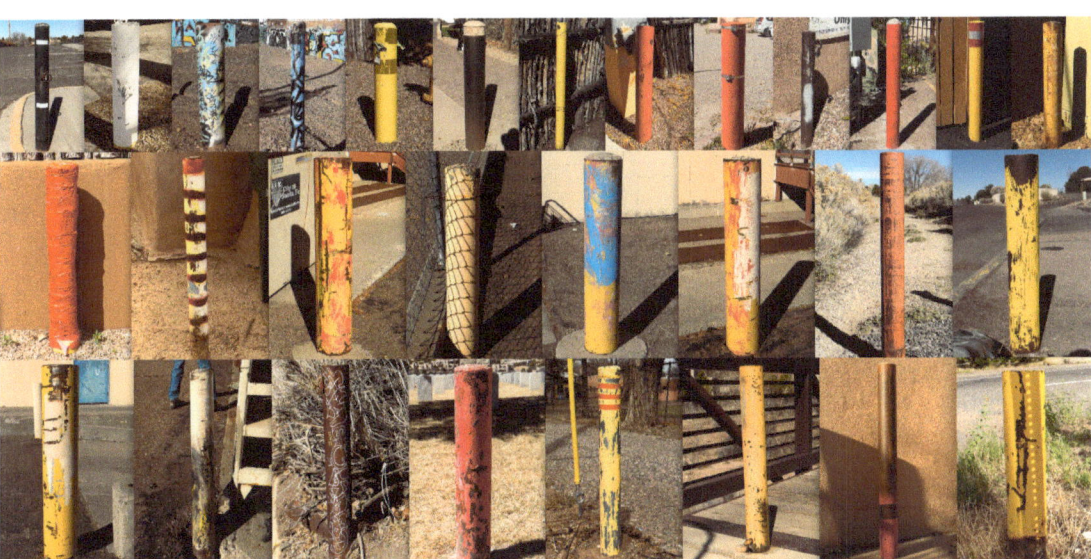

The Online Survey

Many of the survey questions were a variety of "multiple choice" and the results are shown with pie charts and sometimes graphs.

Most of the interesting responses came from multiple choice questions with an option for a written answer.

Other questions simply offered a blank space for a short written answer, and those responses were often the most unexpectedly enthusiastic and revealing.

Filling out a survey seems to be an example of free will within limits: a choice that is fun for some, uncomfortable for others, a possible cause for confusion, challenge, or surprise.

"Why" might be the final question for just about everything.

Multiple choice plus "other" short answer?

puppy ○
screwdriver ○
potato ○

[short answer]

Linear scale single question?

	1	2	3	4	5	6	7	
stupid	○	○	○	○	○	○	○	idiotic

Multichoicegrid one per row?

	something	sumpthin else	whatever	et cetera
ha ha	○	○	○	○
ho ho	○	○	○	○
hee hee	○	○	○	○

Checkbox grid many many?

	checkcheck	chocking	chuckey	flippy
blah blah	☐	☐	☐	☐
yada yada	☐	☐	☐	☐
blub blub	☐	☐	☐	☐

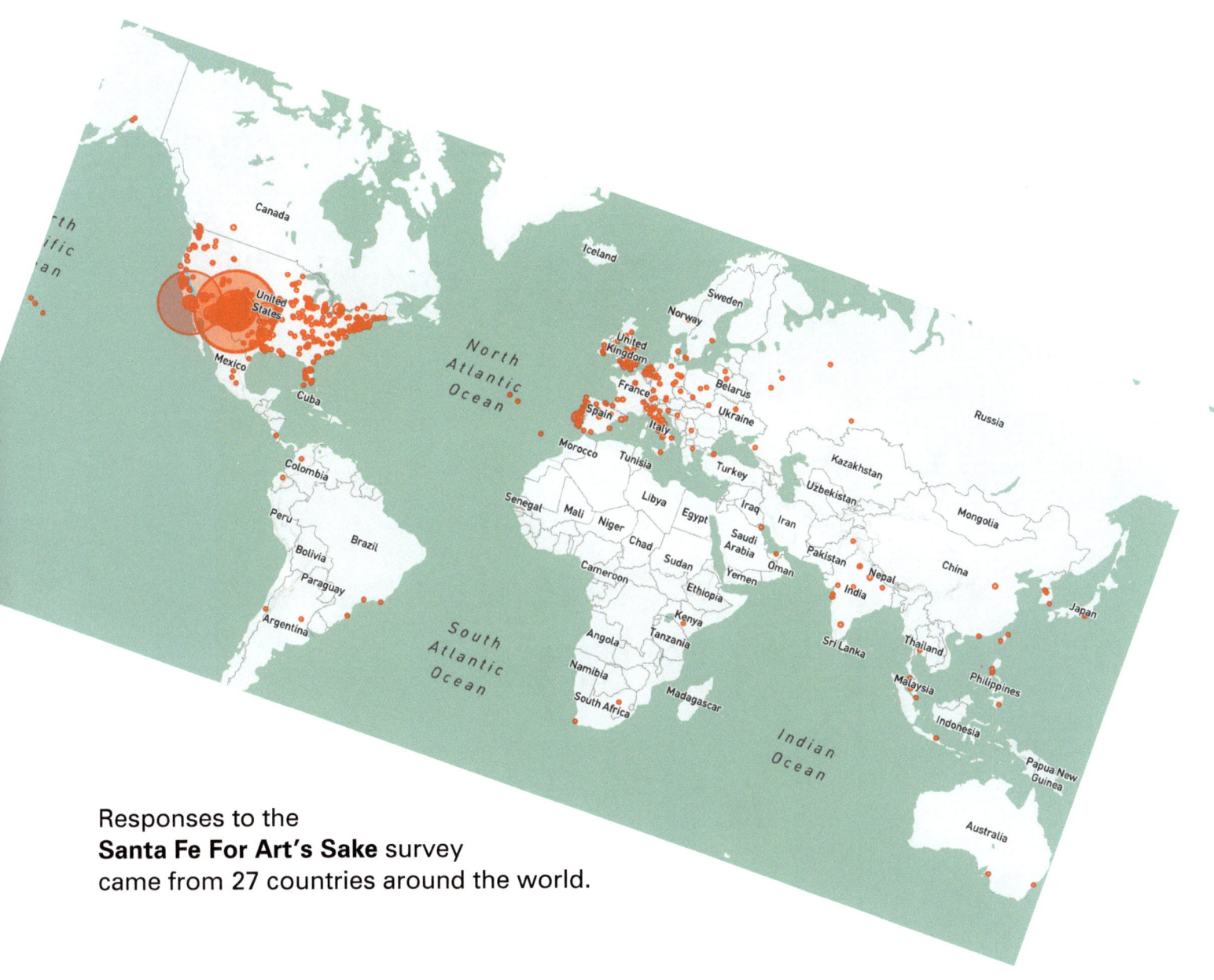

Responses to the
Santa Fe For Art's Sake survey
came from 27 countries around the world.

Which arts organization logos can you recognize?

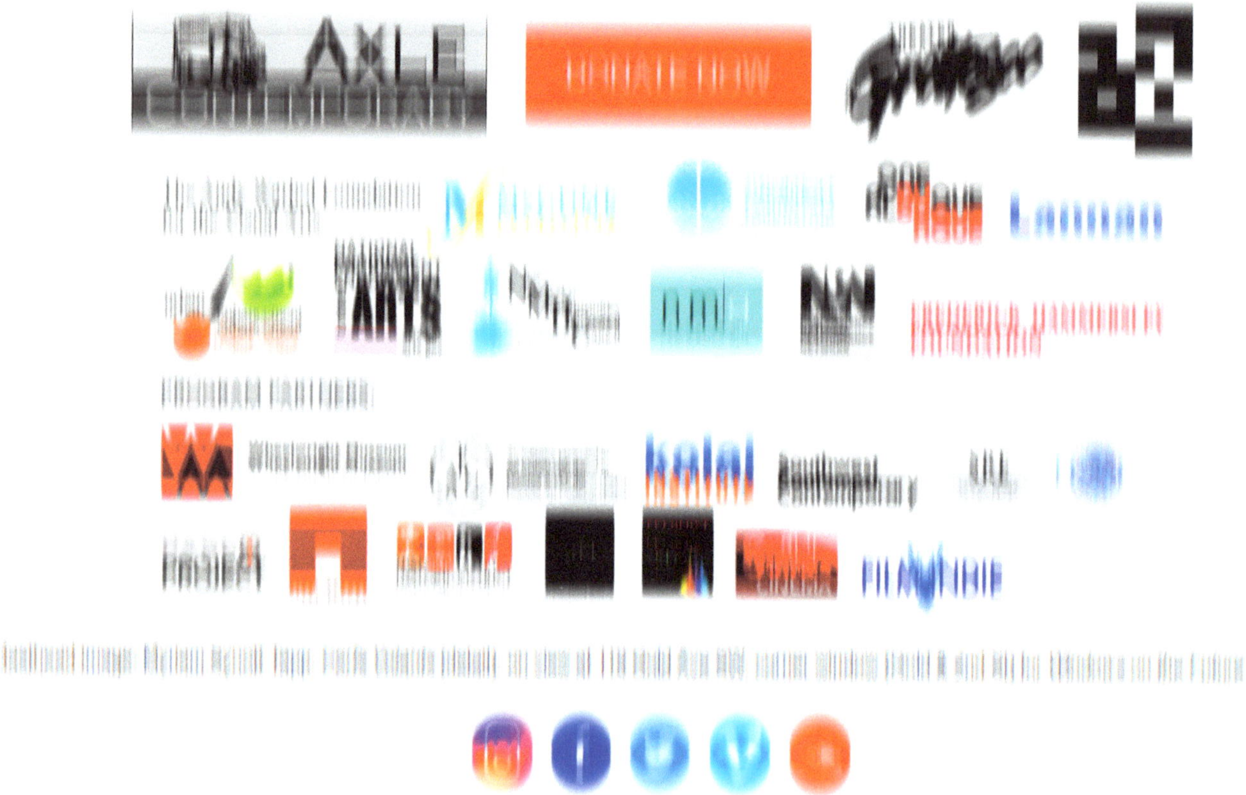

Where do you think the money for this project came from?

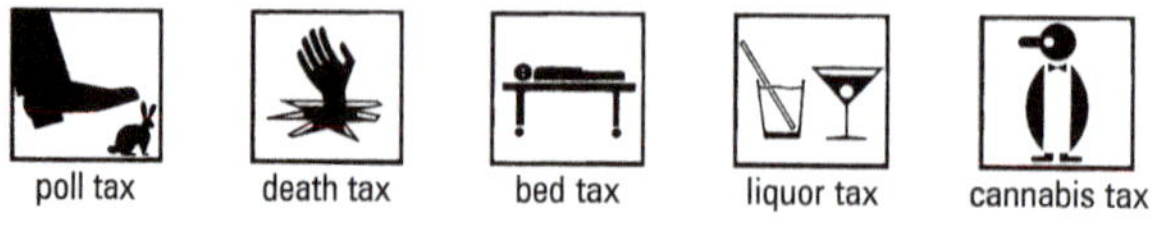

 poll tax
 death tax
 bed tax
 liquor tax
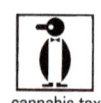 cannabis tax

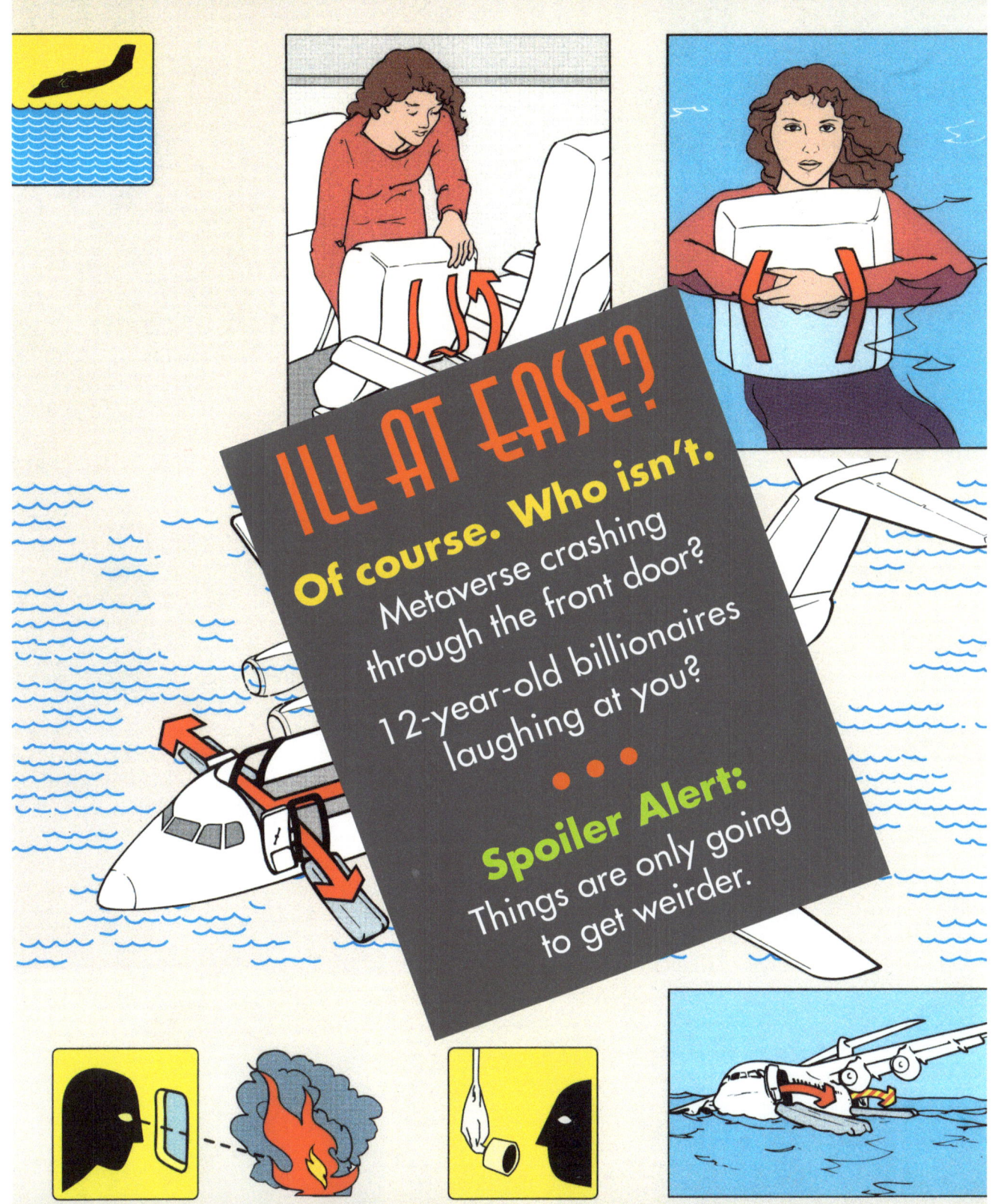

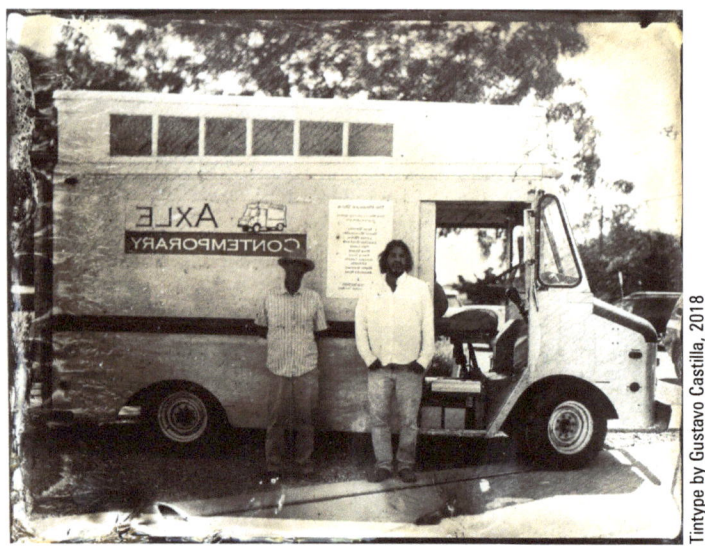

Tintype by Gustavo Castilla, 2018

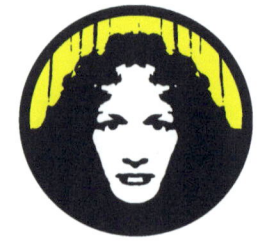 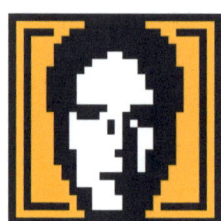

AXLE CONTEMPORARY is a collaborative project by artists Matthew Chase-Daniel and Jerry Wellman. The mobile gallery is an innovative vehicle for arts distribution. Since 2010, it has grown beyond the confines of van/gallery to include book publishing, performance art, and alternative projects for socially engaged art creation and dissemination, exhibiting over 300 New Mexican artists in over 100 exhibitions. Chase-Daniel is a Santa Fe-based artist working primarily in photography and sculpture. His artwork has been exhibited across the U.S. and in Europe, and he has created numerous public art projects. Wellman's paintings and drawings have been exhibited at museums and galleries across the country and his video animation has been presented at national and international festivals.

AxleArt.com

BURNING BOOKS was founded by writer/editor Melody Sumner Carnahan and artist/designer Michael Sumner in 1979 in Oakland, California, to produce art, music, and literature. Since moving to New Mexico in 1989, they continue to publish in obsolete delivery systems: books, posters, discs, pamphlets, and postcards. Artist collaborators include John Cage, Laurie Anderson, Robert Ashley, Steina and Woody Vasulka. The imprint has produced over 35 books and audioworks often with co-publishers—including the Iowa International Writer's Program, Dalkey Archive, Frog Peak Music, as well as museums and institutions, including The Guggenheim, San Francisco Museum of Modern Art, Ars Electronica, and NTT/ICC in Japan.

BurningBooks.org

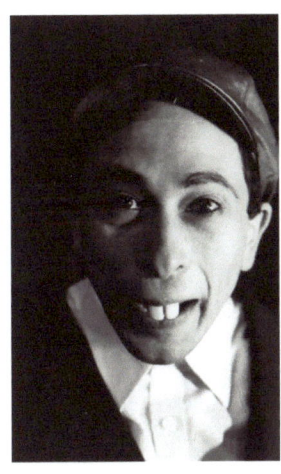 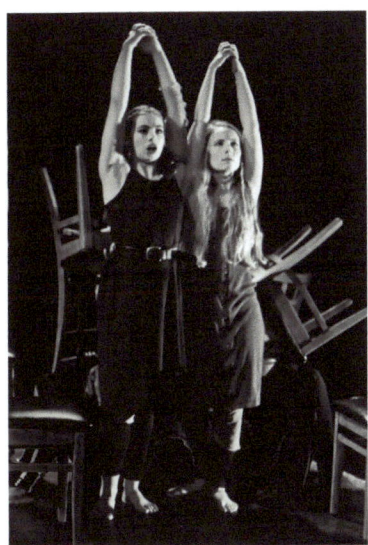 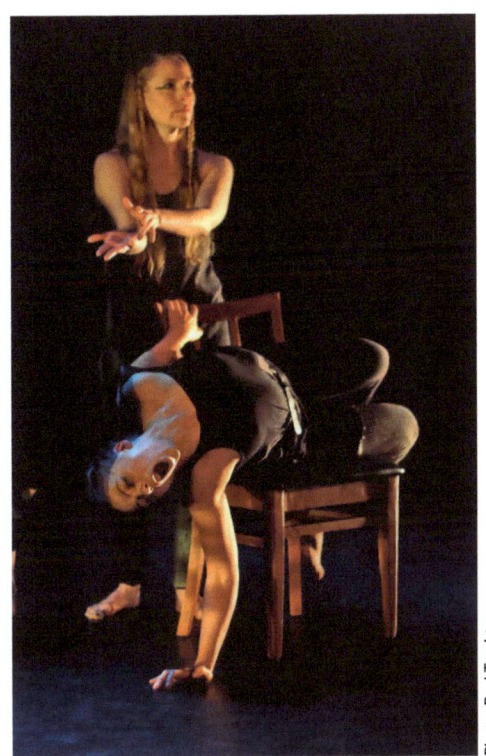

THEATER GROTTESCO began in Paris in 1983 and has created 18 full-length productions and over 50 shorter works ranging in style from Tragic Buffoonery to gesture-based dance. Theater Grottesco has performed in 8 countries, 30 states, most major cities, and dozens of smaller communities. The company was a 2017 National Theatre Project Award winner and has a production that will be permanently archived in the New York Public Library for the Performing Arts. For the *Survey* project, the ensemble is working with an extended research into Physical Greek Chorus. Performed by: Myriah Duda, Koppany Pusztai, Danielle Reddick, Julie Shapiro, and Susan Skeele, with guidance from John Flax.

TheaterGrottesco.org

Photo: Paul Trachtman

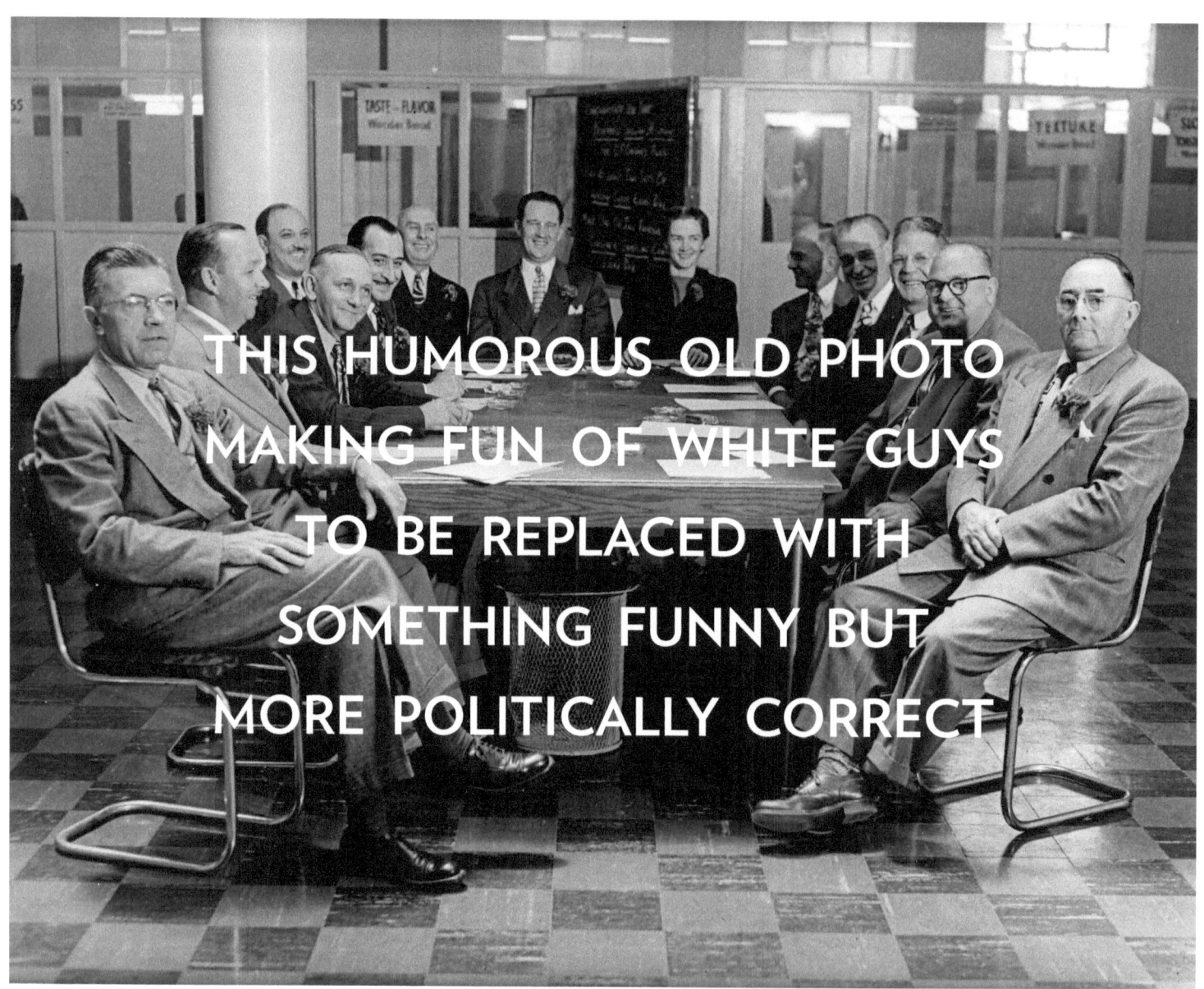

Santa Fe For Art's Sake (the book)
is published by Axle Contemporary in collaboration with Theater Grottesco and Burning Books.

Book Design and Illustration:
Michael Sumner / Burning Books

Editing and Design Assistance:
Melody Sumner Carnahan / Burning Books

© 2022 Axle Contemporary / Theater Grottesco / Burning Books. All rights reserved. No part of this book may be used or reproduced without permission from the publisher. All photographs copyright as credited.

ISBN: 978-1-7369352-5-5

Published and printed in the United States of America.

For information:

AXLE CONTEMPORARY
P.O. Box 22095
Santa Fe, NM 87502
AxleArt.com

BURNING BOOKS
P.O. Box 2638
Santa Fe, NM 87504
BurningBooks.org

THEATER GROTTESCO
1000 Cordova Place #8400
Santa Fe, NM 87505
TheaterGrottesco.org

The "Santa Fe For Art's Sake" project was funded by a Santa Fe Arts & Culture Department– Digital Collaborative Impact Grant, which was granted to Theater Grottesco North America Inc. in collaboration with Axle Contemporary and Burning Books for the period of September 28, 2021 to June 30, 2022.

Supporting and cooperating organizations include: CURRENTS New Media, 516 Arts, Outpost Performance Space, Vital Spaces, form & concept, Reunity Resources, Center, Foto Forum Santa Fe, Center for Contemporary Art, Hecho a Mano, KTRC-Coffee & Culture, City of Santa Fe Economic Development, New Mexico Museum of Art, New Mexico State University Art, NMSA, Moving Arts Española, Dr. Cris Moore of the Santa Fe Institute, Randall Davey Aububon Center & Sanctuary, Santa Fe Fair Grounds.

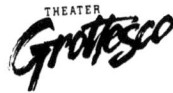 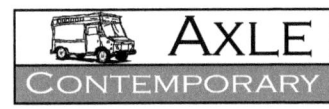 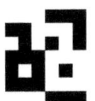

www.ingramcontent.com/pod-product-compliance
Lightning Source LLC
Chambersburg PA
CBHW040408220526

45473CB00004B/1168